What readers are saying about …

SURVIVE THE DAY

"A practical survival guide to bounce back and stand tall when life has knocked you flat. A survival manual for the hurting; you can drop emotional hurts and daily disappointments and replace them with genuine hope."

"This book is a fantastic resource to help Christians in times of suffering and struggle. It provides a real and relatable picture of the hard moments of life and then gives clear and practical steps to give people hope and to start them on the road to healing and wholeness."

"*Survive the Day* gives great tips and encouragement on how to overcome a very difficult struggle in your life. The author, having gone through a very difficult time himself, includes many personal stories and analogies to help encourage readers."

"This is a practical tool to help break the surface of the crashing waves. When you find yourself drowning and need a hand up, this book will give you that hand."

"It is part memoir, part instructions dealing with pain. It will allow you to start the journey of dealing with the storms of life. You will be invited to do it one day at a time."

"A step-by-step guide to climbing out of your despair to rediscover contentment in your life. Essentials for releasing your emotional pain and finding your 'sweet spot' of joy. The end of your rope: The END of Striving … the BEGINNING of your 'New Life'!"

SUR
VIVE
THE
DAY

BEN YOUNG

SUR VIVE THE DAY

THRIVING in the MIDST of LIFE'S STORMS

DAVID C COOK

transforming lives together

SURVIVE THE DAY
Published by David C Cook
4050 Lee Vance Drive
Colorado Springs, CO 80918 U.S.A.

Integrity Music Limited, a Division of David C Cook
Brighton, East Sussex BN1 2RE, England

The graphic circle C logo is a registered trademark of David C Cook.

The website addresses recommended throughout this book are offered as a
resource to you. These websites are not intended in any way to be or imply an
endorsement on the part of David C Cook, nor do we vouch for their content.

Details in some stories have been changed to protect
the identities of the persons involved.

Bible translation credits appear at the end of the book. The author
has added italics to Scripture quotations for emphasis.

Library of Congress Control Number 2020935412
ISBN 978-0-7814-1464-7
eISBN 978-0-8307-8125-6

Published in association with the literary agency
of The Fedd Agency, Inc., Austin, TX

The Team: Michael Covington, Alice Crider, Stephanie Bennett,
Megan Stengel, Jack Campbell, Susan Murdock
Cover Design: Jon Middel
Cover Photo: Getty Images

Printed in the United States of America
First Edition 2020

1 2 3 4 5 6 7 8 9 10

052920

To Nicole and Claire

CONTENTS

11 PART ONE: THE CHALLENGE TO MOVE FORWARD

13 CHAPTER ONE   WHAT ABOUT BOB?

23 CHAPTER TWO   DROWNING TODAY

35 CHAPTER THREE   FAILURE PLUS

49 CHAPTER FOUR   YOUR SHADOW VOICE

63 PART TWO: THE CHOICE TO MOVE FORWARD

65 CHAPTER FIVE   WHEN THE PAIN REMAINS

79 CHAPTER SIX   CHOOSING GOD'S JIU-JITSU

93 CHAPTER SEVEN   UNEXPECTED LOVE

113 CHAPTER EIGHT   ESTAMOS CONTENTOS

129 PART THREE: THE CHANGE TO MOVE FORWARD

131 CHAPTER NINE   WIN THE MORNING

147 CHAPTER TEN   SILENCING YOUR SHADOW VOICE

165 CHAPTER ELEVEN   STOP COMPARING

179 CHAPTER TWELVE   TEN ESSENTIALS FOR SURVIVAL

189 GOING DEEPER

197 ACKNOWLEDGMENTS

199 NOTES

203 BIBLE CREDITS

PART ONE

THE CHALLENGE TO MOVE FORWARD

CHAPTER ONE

WHAT ABOUT BOB?

*"Life is like riding a bicycle. To keep your
balance, you must keep moving."*

Albert Einstein

When you meet someone on a plane or at a party, you typically ask the person three questions: What is your name? Where are you from? What do you do?

The first two questions are easy. My name is Ben Young and I'm from Houston. The third question is a bit tricky. I could say, "I'm a writer" or "I'm a professor." Those are interesting jobs that often open doors to various conversations. People are curious about what you write about or the subject you teach. Another response I could give would be, "I'm an evangelical preacher," which is a conversation stopper, a closed door in the face. It's a surefire signal to insert earphones and check out. No one wants to carry on a conversation with a "preacher" on a long flight.

Perhaps a better way to describe what I do would be to say, "I'm a professional crisis manager."

For the past three decades, I've worked with families and individuals struggling to cope with the harsh realities of major life crisis. I'm a first responder when they receive a diagnosis of a terminal illness, when they've lost a loved one to suicide, when a family is in the long-term battle and heartache of addiction, or when someone close to them was killed in a violent crime. Divorce, mental illness, and depression come across my desk on a regular basis. I never know what life storm will come my way when I pick up the phone or read the next text. Each and every call is heartbreaking, and I count it a privilege to walk through some of life's most jarring moments with those struggling to make it through the day.

More than likely, you picked up this book because you're in the middle of a major life crisis. Someone you love left you with a house full of kids to raise alone. You've received a life-threatening diagnosis that requires long-term medical intervention. Your son relapsed and is out on the street again. You've lost your job and are struggling to pay the bills. You feel afraid, devastated, and hopeless. You wonder how in the world you're going to make it through this relentless storm that seems to only get worse with every passing day. I know what it's like because I've been there.

One of my closest friends is a gifted psychologist. We've known each other for about thirty years, were roommates in college, and have collaborated on several different projects in our careers. We live in different cities, but over the miles and years we've made an effort to get together for a meal once in a while. I would often show up at his office before one of our lunches and plop myself down on his couch, demanding, "Fix me." During these visits, we would joke about the movie *What about Bob?* starring Bill Murray as the neurotic OCD patient Bob Wiley, who consistently becomes addicted to his therapists.

There is a classic scene from the movie when Bob first meets his new psychiatrist, Leo Marvin (played by Richard Dreyfuss). He sits across from Dr. Marvin and, after describing his myriad phobias, screams a chorus of cusswords and obscenities to fake having Tourette's syndrome. In his showcase of fears and neediness, he even feigns cardiac arrest and then begins talking about his divorce while lying on the floor. I asked my friend, "Have you ever had a client do that, lie down on the floor during a session?" He calmly responded, "Yes, I have." Little did I know that some years later I would find myself on the floor of a therapist's office crying my eyes out because it felt like my life was completely over.

During that horrific season of my life, I felt like Bob Wiley. Needy. Afraid. Unable to make it through a single day without begging someone to help me. I had two different therapists on speed dial. Every Monday morning, I had a standing 8:00 a.m. appointment with a counselor, and every Friday, I had another appointment with a clinical psychologist. I needed both. I needed a lot. I called my counselor during off hours, one time taking him away from his daughter's birthday party. I had become Bob, and it felt so shameful and embarrassing. But I was desperate. I was drowning. And I had to reach out for help.

My goal for several weeks, months, and truly years was just to survive the day. "One day at a time," as they say in recovery groups. Every day I battled to make it to 8:30 p.m. when I could hopefully fall asleep naturally without the aid of vitamin A (Ambien). But most nights I needed some help overriding my anxious thoughts to get to sleep.

How I morphed into the Bob character and ended up on the floor of my counselor's office would require a novel-length explanation. We all have our sad stories, and I will come back to mine as this book unfolds. But trust me, as the old television commercial put it, "I'm not just the president of the Hair Club for Men; I'm also a client."

Of course, it's not really the Hair Club. It's the Pain Club. When fear floods your heart every waking moment, when you feel so depressed that you can barely pull yourself out of bed, when your anger boils through the pores of your skin because of the unfairness and injustices of life, you've become a member too. Live long enough and we all find ourselves in this same Pain Club. The question is not *if* you will be a member, but *when* and for *how long?* Some days the pain feels so heavy and intense that we struggle to just carry on.

We all have our life storms, our crises that qualify us for this club no one wants to join. I've discovered we cannot control the relentless storms that rain down pain and frustration on our lives, but the one thing we can control is our response. We can control the choices we make that help us survive the storm. These choices will make us or break us.

I've discovered we **CANNOT CONTROL** the **RELENTLESS STORMS** that rain down **PAIN** and **FRUSTRATION** on our lives, but the one thing we **CAN CONTROL** is **OUR RESPONSE**.

Imagine you're standing on the banks of a wide, raging river. All you want to do is make it to the opposite riverbank, but the rocks, the crocs, and the current keep you stuck right where you are. You have no idea how you will get to the other side. But then you notice some people on the far bank. People just like you who've weathered this same predicament. They've waded through the same river, been snapped at by the crocodiles, and been nearly pulled downstream over the waterfall. They made difficult choices along the way, good choices and bad choices. And yet somehow they are standing on the other bank now. They've navigated that rough water. They can tell you where to step and point out dangers to avoid along the way. If you listen to them, they will guide you to the other side.

Over many painful years I received life-saving words of advice, encouragement, and hope from experienced guides who helped me get to the other side of that river. I am grateful for the many counselors, writers, and wise mentors who spoke the truth in love to me when I needed to hear it. I am not some flawless hero or super Christian guy who made all the right choices and was so full of faith that nothing could stop me when storms bore down on my life with unceasing regularity. I am far from that. But I have listened to and learned from others who have gone before me. And they shared time-tested strategies on how to endure and thrive in the midst of life's storms taking it one day at a time.

This book is about how to survive those days. Not just survive the day by hook or crook, but to survive the day in a way that allows you to draw from the strength and power of God. It will empower you to survive the day in a way that makes you stronger, wiser, and more at peace. *Survive the Day* is not a *Why, God?* book, but a *What Next, God?* book. What do you do next in light of the life storm that's hit you? How do you respond to the difficult challenges and relentless circumstances that surround you again and again?

Survive the Day gives you effective strategies that can help you make it through each day and navigate the challenges in your life storm. These tools will help you feel open, empowered, and more at peace to face the turbulent waters. No matter how long the storm winds blow, these guidelines will help you not only survive but get you to a place where you are thriving again. When you find yourself in circumstances beyond your control, that's when you start to connect to God on a deeper level than you ever imagined. Pain has a way of stripping the layers of pretense and complacency to force you into the presence of God. C. S. Lewis accurately said of pain, "It is [God's] megaphone to rouse a deaf world." It's in these moments that you feel and experience God in a way that you never knew was possible as you choose to access the strength and revitalization that only He can give.

Here's where we are going—or, here's how we will attack it: *Part 1: The Challenge to Move Forward* looks at the various ways we strive to survive. We will meet our enemy called the Shadow Voice, who threatens to take us down and keep us stuck. *Part 2: The Choice to Move Forward* will introduce how humility, grace, and surrender can ground your day in God and His purposes for your life. You will get the tools you need not only to make it through each day but to have the confidence that you'll survive and even thrive. *Part 3: The Change to Move Forward* unpacks how to apply these concepts on a day-to-day basis and how to deal with the debilitating internal dialogue that attempts to drag you back into the mire of your past.

The final chapter gives you ten essentials to daily survival, which will help you build momentum to bring positive changes to your life. The chapters in this book are short for a reason. During a crisis you simply don't have a lot of extra time when life is pounding you to the ground. That's why I included a brief Survival Prayer, Survival Passage, and Survival Practice at the end of every chapter; these are spiritual and practical tools to help you survive and thrive in the moment.

You will meet some fellow survivors in the pages ahead. They will help you glean insights as they have weathered brutal storms of all kinds, including physical pain, parenting special-needs children, drug addictions, cancer bouts, divorce, and the loss of a child. They are my survival mentors, and they will soon be your survival mentors too. These men and women are in the grandstands cheering us on. They speak to us and fill us with courage and power to follow God in the midst of our difficult circumstances.

We're going to pursue this challenge with every ounce of energy, passion, and grit we have inside of us. We're going to give up all the reasons for why we can't have a wonderful life and discover a new and different kind of wonderful. Let's wade in the water together, following the True Professional Crisis Manager who will see us through. And the only way to get to the other side of that riverbank is to get in the water. You are going to make it through this. You are not alone. Let's get after it.

SURVIVAL PRAYER:

Oh God, I thank You for this new day. Help me to receive and apply the tools and strategies I will encounter in the following pages. I surrender my life to You today.

SURVIVAL PASSAGE:

> Dear brothers and sisters, I have not achieved it, but I focus on this one thing: Forgetting the past and looking forward to what lies ahead, I press on to reach the end of the race and receive the heavenly prize for which God, through Christ Jesus, is calling us.

Philippians 3:13–14 (NLT)

SURVIVAL PRACTICE:

Take a walk, and as you're walking, thank God out loud for everything that comes to your mind and the power to move forward today.

CHAPTER TWO

DROWNING TODAY

"You must determine where you are going in your life, because you cannot get there unless you move in that direction. Random wandering will not move you forward."

Jordan B. Peterson

I love the ocean. It is my favorite place to be. It's a wonderful world filled with immense beauty, mystery, and danger. As a surfer, my goal is to catch a great wave. The key to catching the ultimate ride is found in the ability to read waves. Waves come in sets. Sometimes two to three at a time, or in some big sets, four to five waves will roll in one after another. That's fine when you're safely balanced on your board, waiting for just the right wave to ride. It's a different story when you're caught off guard by a rogue wave.

Pummeled by a powerful wave one beautiful November day, I was thrown to the bottom of the ocean, tossed around like a rag doll. I told myself, *Just relax. Stay calm.* I finally found my way back to the surface, gasping for air, only to be hit immediately by a second wave. Down to the bottom again, tumbling, somersaulting, another breathless fight toward the light. I heard the mantra in my head, *Stay calm. Relax.* Wave three pounded me before I could fill my lungs again. It was bad. It was real. My muscles tightened. I started to panic. My arms felt like noodles and my oxygen was depleted. I reached the point where I was about to give up and let go. I thought, *This is what it's like to drown. Now I get it.* I didn't know how I would survive the next wave.

Surfers use many colorful names to describe what happened to me that November day: "getting worked," "taking a few on the head," and "getting a beatdown." Mercifully, I made it out of the water alive. I will come back to explain how in a bit.

The ocean, like life, possesses the power to humble you and overwhelm you beyond measure. Often before our feet hit the floor in the morning, we are already overwhelmed by the day ahead. The stresses of life pound down on us like waves, and sometimes it feels we can barely catch a breath. We feel inundated by the number of tasks we must complete in a day. We feel plagued by finances, by traffic, by technology, and by the tedious nature of our jobs. We feel astounded by our kids and the upside-down, toxic culture they're growing up in. We feel exhausted by the constant juggling act forced upon us by this chaotic, uber-busy, hyper-connected world we all live in.

But feeling overwhelmed is relative. It's one thing to stress about closing the next deal at work or worry about your kids getting into the right college. It's another thing to see your son fall into the clutches of a drug addiction, to hear the news that your teenage daughter is pregnant, to get the horrific call from the police that there's been an accident, or to discover your spouse is having an affair. This level of pain and chaos throws us into survival mode. The trauma, complication, and heartache can seem insurmountable. We wonder how in the world we will make it through the day, and the next day, when we fear life will only get worse. We feel like we're drowning. Fear floods our hearts and we wonder if the turmoil will ever end. As problems, pain, and worries engulf our lives, we cry out to God for help.

THE KEY TO SURVIVING THE DAY

Life is too short and our time is too precious to dwell on why this is all happening to us. Contemplating why we're drowning and receiving such a beatdown misses the point and falls short of the goal, which is to paddle to safety. Now, I'm not attempting to explain why bad things happen to good people or, equally as troubling, why good things happen to bad people. How to reconcile the reality of pain and suffering with the reality of an all-powerful and all-knowing God is one of the most profound and difficult questions we can ever ask. I attempted to tackle these questions in previous books.[1]

Some sources (and well-meaning people) will offer you a simple formula—a spiritual "Get out of jail free" card on how to get God to change your fate right now. They'll spell it out for you in easy steps that guarantee God will perform a miracle in your life today. But I don't buy into "Deus ex machina," god in the

LIFE IS TOO SHORT

and **OUR TIME IS TOO**

PRECIOUS to dwell

on **WHY THIS IS ALL**

HAPPENING TO US.

machine, like in the movies when some magical resolution happens, or God shows up in a flash and makes everything better at the last minute. I do believe God shows up, at certain times and seasons, in a supernatural way and changes the course of human history. He even swoops down and performs a miracle that saves the day on occasion. I celebrate the fact that God does intervene to heal, to deliver, and to guide us in unexpected ways, but that's an exception and not the rule. Most of the time God allows the wheel of cause and effect and free will to have its way without a "parting of the Red Sea" event. I believe the supernatural sustaining power of God in the midst of real life storms is an underrated miracle that deserves more press than we give it.

The key to surviving the day, in my experience, can be found within the resources God provides for us. When the waves of pain and chaos hit your life, it feels disorienting and debilitating. Fighting through this becomes an emotional, physical, and spiritual battle, yet God does provide *what* we need *when* we need it. He has the power to inspire us to move forward in a way that will keep us open, strong, and free, regardless of whether our circumstances improve or not.

We all go through dark, difficult seasons that we feel may never end. Waves of pain and chaos flood our world and overwhelm us. As brutal as these storms may be, we always have a choice. We have the choice to cave in to the chaos and craziness or to choose the hard thing and allow God to transform us through the trials.

Whatever your storm may be at this moment, I know that God has not forgotten you. No matter the fear, the anger, the pain, or the despair, God is still with you and He will empower you to make it through. You are not alone. This agonizing storm is also an opportunity for God to do a deep work in your heart and life. There are men and women on the other side who have made it through the storm you are going through right now. They can help you make it through; I can help you make it through. We can make it through together in order to see a better tomorrow.

During the *What about Bob?* time in my life, when I found myself on the floor crying out to God, my therapist, and maybe those who could hear me in the waiting room, I knew I didn't have the tools to survive on my own. I looked to many places for help. Friends, family, and even philosophers played a major role in my rescue and recovery.

DISORIENTED AND LONGING FOR HOME

French philosopher Paul Ricoeur viewed life as a series of three movements.[2] First, there's what he calls *orientation*. The time in our lives when things feel right, good, and peaceful. Put simply, we feel at home. Second is the movement that leads to *disorientation*. A life-altering event occurs, a catastrophe strikes, and we feel disoriented. Life has radically changed. We now live in this space of disorientation and long to return "home," but that home no longer exists. Third, there's *reorientation*. The realization of the "new normal." After the pain, struggle, and endurance we learn in disorientation, we find ourselves in a place of reorientation. It feels like home in some ways, but in other ways it's entirely different.

Once we've been hit by the wave of cancer, the wave of death, the wave of divorce, or some other life-changing tragedy, we are forced to enter a new, unfamiliar life—we're disoriented. We can't go back to the old life; it's gone. We have to move forward into this new life, with all of its pain, pressure, and mystery. Søren Kierkegaard's iconic quote comes to mind, "Life can only be understood backwards, but it must be lived forwards."[3]

Perhaps you're currently in the space of disorientation. Maybe a bomb went off in your life that led you to a time of dislocation, confusion, and chaos. You may have been blindsided by loss, disappointment, or tragedy, and now your new reality feels fragile. I know that experience well myself. In writing this book, I dove into my old journals and relived some of the excruciating moments of pain, uncertainty, and despair. I read prayers and poems that poured out of me during my own dark season of disorientation that helped me process the pain and draw near to God.

As I read and reflected on my personal journal, I noticed a theme, a headline, or a quote on nearly every page: "FORWARD MOTION." It was a reminder to keep moving forward no matter what happens, no matter the pain, no matter what you face—keep moving forward. I put Kierkegaard's message in front of me on a daily basis: live life forward. Nietzsche's words encouraged me, "That which doesn't kill us outright only makes us stronger." Paul's words in Philippians 3:13 were a great source of hope, "One thing I do: forgetting what lies behind and reaching forward to what lies

I believe the

SUPERNATURAL

SUSTAINING POWER

OF GOD in the midst of

REAL LIFE STORMS is an

UNDERRATED MIRACLE

that **DESERVES MORE**

PRESS THAN WE GIVE IT.

ahead" (NASB). These words stayed in my heart and mind through-out the day. I would meditate on them and speak them out loud in the car as I was driving to work. I put them in a prominent place on my cell phone so I would never lose sight of this pressing need to move forward each day.

One of the most helpful strategies to making it through the day was and still is this concept of forward motion. When the undercurrent of your life pulls you backward or in circles, you have to fight to move forward. The goal here is to keep moving through this stage of disorientation you're in now until you get to the stage of reorientation. The enemy, your emotions, and your circumstances conspire against you to keep you down and stuck. Even though it's been a decade since that dark, brutal season in my life, I still fight to keep my eyes focused on the power to move forward one day at a time and not allow myself to listen to the voices that will drag me back into the dark cave of disorientation. The fact that you bought this book and are reading these words is a step in the right direction. Every chapter of this book is designed to keep you moving forward one day at a time, building on the strength God gives you and embracing this new life ahead. But how do we move forward when we are in such dire straits? When the undertow threatens to take us down?

Going back to my predicament in the ocean—you know, the drowning thing, the beatdown … When I was in crisis, being pummeled by wave after wave, I reached a moment when my oxygen was depleted, my strength was waning, and I was about to give up. But out of the corner of my eye, I saw a guy not too far away on a stand-up paddleboard (SUP). It's a bit ironic since for years I mocked SUP guys, calling them sweepers, and the janitors of the ocean, with their big brooms stroking back and forth. But this was not the time for surfer's sarcasm. I was literally drowning. So I did something I had never done before in the ocean. I raised my hand out of the water and cried out, "Help! I need some help over here!"

He quickly recognized I was caught in a rip current, and he knew better than to get himself in the same danger by coming in after me where we would then both be helplessly stuck. But from his vantage point he could see where the current was going. He could see how I could get out and gave me instruction on which direction to move so that the current would carry me out of harm's way.

"Paddle fifteen yards to your left and it will take you back out," he yelled. I dug down deep and discovered I had a few more strokes in me. I followed his advice and paddled those precious fifteen yards to the left and escaped with my life intact. I was so grateful to have survived my brush with death.

I would have drowned that day if I had not asked for help. I would not be alive today if it were not for the help that SUP guy gave me in that moment. Likewise, I would also not be here today had I not cried out for help from some gifted therapists and trusted friends when I was drowning in my personal sea of hurt and pain. When you are in trouble, you must get help from others. You will not make it through without the wise counsel you can get from people who know your situation and have been through it themselves. When we are in so deep that we can't see our own way out, we need others who can see where we are and, with a better perspective and wisdom, give us guidance to make it out of harm's way. A major step in moving forward today will be to access the help you need from someone else.

Coming up next, we will dive into both the effective choices and the ineffective choices we make as we attempt to move forward into smoother waters.

SURVIVAL PRAYER:

Father, You know the storm I'm in right now. Fear, anxiety, and worry find me everywhere I turn. Give me the strength to turn to You and the wisdom to make solid choices. Help me to move forward and to stay open to You throughout this day.

SURVIVAL PASSAGE:

> Forgetting what lies behind and reaching forward
> to what lies ahead, I press on toward the goal for
> the prize of the upward call of God in Christ Jesus.
> *Philippians 3:13–14 (NASB)*

SURVIVAL PRACTICE:

Make an appointment to seek help and wise counsel today. Find a trusted mentor, pastor, or counselor who can help.

CHAPTER THREE

FAILURE PLUS

*"Success is not final, failure is not fatal: it is
the courage to continue that counts."*
Winston Churchill

My junior high school in South Carolina was a dump. It was called
Dent. Yes, Dent Junior High School. Can't make it up. The name
couldn't have been more fitting. In the locker room, rusty nails
served as hooks where we hung our clothes, and the toilet stalls had
no doors. In ninth grade, I tried out for the basketball team and
made the final cut. But I sat on the bench for most of the year as the
third-string point guard. I didn't even have an official uniform. The
staff would toss me the leftover ones from years past or the ones that
didn't fit anyone else. One of the uniforms I wore had a huge blue
ink stain on it. I guess it didn't matter because I never got to play in
the games anyway. Our coach's real job was on the football field, but
the school was so poor, he was required to coach basketball as well.
He was an intimidating fella with a booming voice.

One of my strongest memories that season was report-card day—the dreaded day when the coach asked everyone to bring our report cards in so he could check our grades. My teammate Ronald was scared to death about giving his report card to the coach. Ronald had failed a class and was worried about how our coach would respond, but he casually handed in his card anyway. Coach Simmons opened Ronald's card and began to scan his grades. Then in a burst of laughter, Coach yelled out, "*F-plus!* What's an *F-plus?*" My friend Ronald had the ingenious idea of trying to pretty up his F with a plus sign in an attempt to assuage the coach's anger. Well, Ronald's plan backfired and our whole team received the wrath of our beloved coach. F+. That was Ron's strategy—just add a plus sign.

No one likes to fail. Especially in the middle of a crisis, when so much is riding on how you handle the variety of problems coming at you. I've walked alongside many families struggling to cope with a child who's gone off the rails due to an addiction. The parents feel like failures because of the mess their kid created by his or her choice to use and abuse a substance. When a life storm like addiction strikes your life, there is no perfect way to handle it. There's no formula to prevent you from feeling like a failure.

But failure is part of life, and as much as we'd like to avoid it altogether, we can't. We may fail in school, at a job, with our finances, in a relationship, as a parent or spouse. What lies beneath is a deep sense of personal disappointment. We feel we let someone down or we did not measure up to a standard, usually our own. We had high expectations of how our lives would turn out, but now things may look radically different.

When we sense failure on the horizon, our minds go into over-drive to prevent the disaster, reverse the damage, and change our outcome. In my life, I tried to let the chips fall where they may at times, but for months on end, I attempted to catch those chips and glue them back together. I could not afford to fail. Failure scared me, so I would try to add something like a plus sign. I responded with every counteractive move I could think of to change the situation and fix the problem. For me this was a time of disorientation and I was desperate to find solutions and answers that would fix my life so I could return to that place of orientation and my idea of normality. I discovered that when you're drowning, failing, and flailing, you'll try all means necessary to get your life back.

When faced with a life storm that is whirling and spinning in so many directions, we try anything to gain a sense of stability and control.

We plan out a strategy for how to fix our problems. We search online for "How to get out of hell and live to tell about it." We write down the best solutions. We find and make an action plan. We meet with the smartest people on the planet—the fixers, the doctors, the lawyers, the financial planners, and the psychologists. We trust that with their insight and counsel we can mop our way out of the mess.

Now don't get me wrong; I believe it's a wise move to consult the experts and build sound strategies to manage problems in life, but doing so won't necessarily change our circumstances. But, hey, if that does solve all your problems and win the day, then please put down this book and write your own. I will be delighted to write the foreword for your book. We stay unhealthy when we try to control others around us, especially in the name of "helping" them. We have to know when we cross the line from influencing others to controlling them, which we like to call "helping."

During this time of suffering, disappointment, and disorientation, our emotions erupt in a new and intense way. I'm a typical guy in many ways, but I also tend to be a more analytical person who spends a lot of time in my head thinking and reflecting. I am not that good at expressing my emotions. However, during this rugged season of my life, this season of disorientation when my life exploded into a million pieces, my emotions continually dominated my world. I experienced a depth and intensity of emotions that I never knew possible. Not only did I feel like a failure, I also felt a deep sense of unresolved anger. One day I ran into my friend Jim, who is one of the most sincere and godly men in our city. As he usually does, he asked me, "How can I pray for you?" I said, "Pray that I don't hit someone." He looked puzzled at my response, so I further explained, "Pray that I don't hit someone because that is not going to help my situation at all." He absorbed my response and then simply nodded in agreement.

Anger. Rage. Just another way we respond to the overwhelming nature of a bad day that will not go away. We rage internally and externally. We get mad at what our lives have become or why we have to deal with this grim and grueling situation. We look around and feel like everyone else is walking around all happy and smiling without a care in the world. It's probably a good time to take a break from social media so we don't buy into the false belief that everyone except us is taking a Caribbean vacation. *Do they ever have to work? What's up with that?* It's not fair, is it?

Now, there's a productive side to anger as well. Sometimes anger can light the fire that helps us get up and move forward, to get unstuck. But hanging on to anger, allowing it to grow inside our hearts, will fester into bitterness and destroy us and the people we love. Anger will not help us to survive the day.

Fear can also flood our lives in times like these. What's going to happen next? How will I cope with that? Can I pay the bills? What if things get worse? In an attempt to deal with our fears, we worry. Worry is a strange, unproductive form of control. We hold on to this insane belief (even subconsciously) that if we stress out about a particular problem in our lives, then somehow, some way, the issue will go away or we'll find a solution. We can't fall asleep because we worry. We wake up in the middle of the night, and we worry. When morning finally comes, we pour ourselves a big ole cup of worry to start our day. We call our family and friends and dump our worries on them. We text our worries to those who we think will care about what we have to say. We may have the underlying thought, *If I didn't love them so much, I wouldn't worry. If I don't worry about them, who will? It's my role to be stressed. My job is to worry and be anxious. This shows how much I care. This proves how much I love. I can't help it—I've always been a worrier.* But this kind of thinking keeps us stuck in our pain and problems. It keeps us from moving forward. Some level of worry is a part of being human—there's no way we can completely stop worrying in this life—but excessive worrying doesn't solve our problems and will not help us survive the day.

On the other end of the spectrum is the positive thinking strategy. Sometimes we try to think positive in order to deal with difficult circumstances and the painful emotions of anger and fear that engulf us. We reason that if we can just remain positive throughout the day, then we will get relief from the pain. There are many names for it. Some call it the Law of Attraction, the power of positive thinking, name it–claim it, blab it–grab it. The theory is that if we believe strongly enough, if we focus on only the best possible outcome, then God will turn our circumstances around. I do believe we should get ahold of our thoughts and muster up a positive attitude and outlook on life. That's healthy in many ways, but it does not mean that God is obligated to make our thoughts a reality (a la the Law of Attraction). Mustering up optimism certainly is not a magic wand that will get us through the day and control our situation.

Prayer is another strategy we use to deal with these emotions and the turbulent circumstances we face. If we pray according to God's will, we expect our prayers to be answered. We pray for healing, we pray for help in our marriage, we pray that our prodigal child will come to his or her senses and find the way home. Hope arises in us and we think, *This is it. God will come through now.* But then things fall apart, and our hope is crushed. When our circumstances don't change, we can feel let down, frustrated, and stuck right back where we started. It's easy to get discouraged when our prayers go unanswered. We silently ask, *What's wrong with me? What's wrong with God? Why doesn't He answer my prayers?*

But we still pray. Boy, do we pray and pray and pray some more. We may fast and we may try to cut deals with God. We promise to do *this* if God will just do *that*. God, change him. God, fix the problem. God, please heal her. God, do something. Of course, God could, but most of the time He does not. Miracles do exist, but they are exceptions to the rule. They're called "miracles" because of their rarity. Hear me on this: I believe in prayer. I believe we absolutely need to pray to make it through every day. Prayer is essential and not optional! But I believe *what we pray* and *how we pray* are vital. I'll explain more on that note later.

I've talked with normal people, I mean really normal people, who out of great suffering and exasperation have gone to see one of those fake television faith healers who knock people on the ground in order to heal them. Driving miles and miles with their sick friend in the back seat so the faith healer in his white sport coat can wave his arms around, then knock over and supposedly heal their friend. Why would a normal person do that? Desperation. I get it. When we are desperate, we will try to find anything, or anyone, that can help. We throw money at the problem. We confront the people surrounding the problem. We make excuses for the person with the problem.

About three years after my initial *What about Bob?* moment on the floor, I had progressed to actually sitting on the couch in my therapist's office. I finally asked him, "Hey, what kind of therapy are you using on me?" I'd been seeing him every week for years now, but I had never thought to ask that question. He said, "Grief therapy. I am trying to move you through the stages of grief." *Oh*, I thought, *dang, this sure is taking a long time.*

DABDA is the famous acrostic used in grief therapy that attempts to describe how we process loss in stages. I like DABDA even though grief does not always progress in five sequential stages. It varies from person to person. The *D* stands for denial. We deny what happened to us or our loss. Some refer to this first stage as shock. The *A* stands for anger. We are mad at the person who's gone, or why he or she is gone, or the circumstance we find ourselves in now. Or we're angry at God for allowing this mess to happen. Anger boils even in nice people. *B* is for bargaining with life or with God to somehow change the situation and return us home to orientation. We try to negotiate a deal and circumvent the grief process. *D* is for depression. We feel empty, overwhelmed, and paralyzed by where we find ourselves—so far away from where we thought we would be in life—and we feel little to no desire to carry on. *A* stands for acceptance—the final grief stage in which we accept what happened to us, and we are finally able to assimilate it into our lives and move forward. Sometimes it takes weeks, months, even years to reach a point of acceptance.

Grieving is part of the process. And it's not all bad. Some men never cry. They pride themselves on not crying. But crying is normal. When my life unraveled, I cried a lot. At one point, it seemed as if I couldn't possibly have any more tears to shed. I cried every morning for days and days in a row. Crying is a gift God has given us to help release our pain and externalize our emotions. Even "Jesus wept." At the same time, we can't cry all day. We have to give ourselves time to grieve, and then we have to find ways to start living and moving forward.

Because we are overwhelmed by the problem, we wake up to it, go to sleep with it, dream about it. Obsessed with turning our upside-down world right-side up again, we grasp at any and every glimmer of hope. But in doing so, we end up missing the only thing we have: today. We miss out on life right now. We miss the chance to respond to God and others today. We miss the joy and hope in the moment and wind up filled with massive amounts of fear, worry, and anger. We get ulcers, lose sleep, struggle with relationships, and experience depression. Trauma and drama may happen in a moment, but the fallout can torment us for a long time.

Some of these responses actually may be somewhat helpful, it's true. There is a place for some of it. We need to be aware of the ways we are coping and our perspective of reality. We have to use our heads and plan what we can do next. We should consult experts for wisdom, pray to God for a rescue. These actions can help, but I do not think they are the sure and easy path to survival.

After we exhaust all of our efforts to fix the problem and make it through the day, we are left feeling weary, overwhelmed, and powerless to change anything. And as bad as it is to fail or feel like a failure, it's failure that teaches us. Failure instructs us to find another way, to take a different path. I know, because I tried all of the unproductive ways. And my guess is you've picked up this book because you've been there too! The good news is you are not alone.

We've all tried to cope in ineffective ways. But I want you to know there is a different way that is life-giving and fulfilling. And what a relief it is.

So much of our time and energy is spent *doing* in an effort to change our circumstances, and we pay little attention to simply *being*. And the truth is there will be times when all of our best and worst efforts will not change our circumstances. Some of us may subconsciously *do more* to avoid just being. When we are still and not distracted with doing, we are alone with our thoughts, fears, and emotions, and there are times in our lives when avoiding this downtime seems more comfortable. In the chapters ahead, we will learn to live in the moment, one day at a time. We will realign our priorities and instead learn to first *be*, which will help us to *do*. The order and emphasis of our focus matter. *Be*, then *do*.

When we stop focusing on the doing first, trying to make everything happen, and start by being, our burden of doing is lightened and we find a peace that passes all understanding. In order to just *be*, you have to get your mind to stop worrying about the future and regretting the past. You learn to "be still and know that God is God" and realize that this very moment is all that's real. This isn't easy because we all have what's known as a "shadow voice" that thwarts our faith and a real enemy that lurks behind the scenes. But there are ways of silencing that voice and defeating our enemy. So where do we begin? It will not be easy because we must face that enemy who does not want us to survive the day.

Let's go back to report-card day. For those of us in a life storm, this is report-card day. This crisis, this storm, can be seen as an

When we **STOP**

FOCUSING on the **DOING**

first, **TRYING TO MAKE**

EVERYTHING HAPPEN,

and **START BY BEING,** our

BURDEN OF DOING is

LIGHTENED and **WE FIND**

A PEACE THAT PASSES

ALL UNDERSTANDING.

ongoing series of tests. I failed many of them. F-plus, mixed in with some Cs and As. But this is much deeper than a test, because your life and the people you deeply love rest in the balance. And it's this testing that makes us stronger. I don't like it. I would trade all this strength and knowledge to have my old, normal life of orientation, feeling at home, but that's not where I am. And it's not where you are. Life deals out all kinds of cards and tests for its players. You've been given a tough hand. But I think we are up to the challenge!

SURVIVAL PRAYER:

God, I feel overwhelmed by the problems I face today. I feel power-less to change this situation. Fill me with the courage to persevere and to live in this moment, and in this day, not tomorrow. Help me to be content with the love and grace You send my way today. I choose to listen to You throughout this day.

SURVIVAL PASSAGE:

> I thank my God every time I remember you. In all my prayers for all of you, I always pray with joy because of your partnership in the gospel from the first day until now, being confident of this, that he who began a good work in you will carry it on to completion until the day of Christ Jesus.

Philippians 1:3–6

SURVIVAL PRACTICE:

Make a list in a notebook or on your cell phone of three things you've tried to do that have not worked. Make another list of three things you've done that have helped you move forward, and do those things today.

CHAPTER FOUR

YOUR SHADOW VOICE

"It is during our darkest moments that we must focus to see the light."
Aristotle

I was having lunch with a friend of mine a couple of months ago. He's a great guy, a devoted dad and loving husband. He has been very successful in his business and is active in church. He's the kind of guy who seems to have the world on a string. But as we talked over burgers and fries, he surprised me with an unexpected story about himself. I knew he had endured a season of brutal storms in his life, but what he told me next was news to me. He said, "You know, a couple years ago I started to have this thought. It just crept into my mind. I don't know if it came up from inside of me, or from the devil, but it was like a voice telling me, *You're not a failure; you just don't measure up. You're not good enough, and time is running out.*"

My friend said when these thoughts started circulating inside his mind, over time, the recurring voice led him into a period of depression that lasted a year. I would have never guessed this sharp, upbeat guy who seemed to have everything in the world going for him had gone through a season like that.

We all have that nagging, condemning voice whispering in our heads at times. It may be subtle and quiet, or it may be loud and obnoxious, but everyone experiences it on occasion. What is that voice, and where does it come from?

Carl Jung was one of the most brilliant and influential psychoanalysts the world has ever seen. He laid the groundwork for analytical psychology that helps break down why we do what we do. Jung believed that human beings have three aspects to them. First, we have a persona. The persona represents the roles and masks we wear to function within society. We may outwardly project attributes such as strength, smarts, wit, or professionalism in our interactions with others. Personas are neither good nor bad, but they make up our coping mechanisms that are necessary for us to navigate life and relationships in this world.

Second, we have an ego. The ego is the aspect of ourselves that gives us a sense of being, identity, and willfulness. The ego is our mind and our will combined, helping us make decisions throughout the day. This use of the word *ego* is not about being egotistical or prideful, but rather being grounded and having a healthy sense of self.

Third, we have a shadow side. The shadow side represents all the conflicting desires, temptations, and bizarre thoughts we all have. The Shadow is the dark side of ourselves we want to hide and keep tucked away in some box in the basement of our being, never to be discovered. Everything that contradicts the persona we want to project is shoved into our personal shadow.[1]

When we are struggling to survive the day, it's the voice of the Shadow that we hear. I do not know the source of this "Shadow Voice" with absolute certainty. Is it our flesh or fallen nature? Is it the voice of the devil and his minions? Is it the dark side of our psyche as Jung described? Even Dr. Jung believed in the reality of evil forces that transcended psychotherapeutic methods. I do not have all the answers, but I do know that this voice, regardless of its source, can wreak havoc on our lives. We are all familiar with this voice.

The Shadow Voice will murmur to us, grumble at us, and keep us distracted from everything but the dark. It is the voice of fear, regret, and shame. It reminds us of past failures and injustices, convincing us that what happened to us is unforgivable and unredeemable. It relentlessly tells us we are insignificant and unworthy. It whispers in our ear, tempting us to keep doing the very things that will only keep us bound to our pain.

The Shadow is the voice that says things like, *You're not a failure; you just don't measure up. You're not good enough, and time is running out.* It prods us to flash the victim card and shirk our responsibility, keeping us from taking effective action or moving forward. It taunts us by suggesting that we will never be able to change our circumstances and there is no hope for our future. Dread and discouragement fill our heart and mind as we imagine just how horrible and painful life will probably be. This deceptive voice seeks to ruin our life today and paralyze us tomorrow.

The Shadow Voice also seeks to isolate us and discourage us from reaching out to accept an offer of help or hope from others. The Voice wants to squash our ambitions and our confidence in our ability to support ourselves and our family. It creates a heaviness and a hopelessness in our life. Despair, depression, and anxiety are all symptoms of this heaviness that threatens to smother and crush us. The Shadow Voice desires to take away our hope. It seeks to crush our hope that we can make it through this day. It robs us of hope that God is still present and working in our life.

So what can we do to silence the Shadow Voice? How can we keep this villain from destroying our life and the lives of the ones we love? It starts with awareness. We need to be aware that the Shadow Voice is real, cunning, and deceitful, and we need to learn to recognize it when it whispers. When we learn to recognize the Shadow Voice, we no longer have to fall for its destructive schemes.

How do we do that? There are some telltale tactics the Shadow Voice uses to sabotage us. When our head and heart are spinning with negative thoughts and painful emotions, it's a good sign that the Shadow Voice is hard at work. We can be sure it's the Shadow Voice talking if our thoughts incite any of these responses.

Typical Tactics of the Shadow Voice

FEAR. Sometimes life gets so tough you don't know what to do. You can be hit relationally, financially, emotionally, or in all of those areas at the same time. You feel the grip of fear squeezing tighter and tighter. You feel vulnerable and unprotected. David in the book of Psalms cried out in fear to God countless times because he felt surrounded by his enemies and he saw no way out. When fear overwhelms you, you can be sure that's the Shadow Voice working against you.

SHAME. The Shadow Voice is masterful at inducing shame by making you feel flawed and defective. Guilt says, "I've *done something* wrong." But shame says, "*I am* wrong." At the heart of many psychological disorders is a deep-seated sense of shame. The Voice says, *If people really knew who you are, they would reject you.* Many of us have recordings in our minds and in our hearts that play the same dirge over and over. *You're not good enough. You're a failure. You're stupid. You're ugly. You don't fit in. You're never going to amount to anything.* We play these messages again and again and again.

Shame makes us feel humiliated and exposed. When it festers in our souls, we either seek to hide and internalize our emotions or we power up and externalize our feelings, often with unhealthy actions. We hide because we feel so unworthy and dirty. Or we power up in an attempt to present an impeccable front of invulnerability. Sometimes we just cave in to the shame and plunge ourselves into a lifestyle that we know is way off the good path—but we feel we can't go home after all we've done and who we've become.

REGRET. The Shadow Voice loves to pull you back into the room of "if onlys." If only I hadn't taken that drink. If only I hadn't chosen to marry him. If only I had done more to love my child. If only I hadn't taken that risk. If only I had prayed more. Regret is a powerful force that makes us dwell on what happened and what could have been. It's like trying to drive your car forward by staring in your rearview mirror … you will crash.

When you catch yourself living in the room of "if onlys," you can be sure it's the Shadow Voice that lured you in.

SELF-INDULGENCE. When the pressure of life and facing the day seems too much, the Shadow Voice whispers, *You deserve this. Life dealt you a bad hand, so do whatever you want to do that makes you feel happy.* Of course, we need to take care of ourselves and our own needs when experiencing a major crisis, but this is not the same thing. This is when we are tempted to indulge our base appetites for pleasure through drugs, sex, drinking, overeating, shopping, or traveling. Most of these are escape hatches or, to mix metaphors here, a type of anesthesia to numb the pain of life. This temptation to indulge or self-medicate only leads to heartache, addiction, and more pain.

SELF-PITY. One of the most common ways the Shadow Voice speaks into our lives is through the language of victimhood. Self-pity makes us wallow in our misery and circumstances, feeling sorry for ourselves. It causes us to point the finger and blame someone or something else for our predicament. Self-pity is a way to elicit sympathy from others and deflect responsibility for our own lives. At times victims do have the right to scream, "What happened to me was unfair. I did nothing to deserve this. It was not my fault!" And while that may be true, adopting a victim identity instead of rising to take responsibility will only do further damage.

The Shadow Voice has a goal in all of this. Through all of these tactics of fear, shame, regret, self-indulgence, and self-pity, the Shadow Voice seeks to keep us ineffective, nonproductive, and powerless. When we listen to the lies and fall for the schemes, if we believe what the Shadow Voice says is true, we will end up feeling *afraid, alone,* and *hopeless.* Those emotions often result in our feeling trapped in our dilemma with no way out and nowhere to go. And that's the ultimate goal of this insidious Voice—to stop us from moving forward in our lives. To keep us *stuck*. When that happens, the Shadow Voice has won. When my life was starting to unravel, the voice of fear and shame were always lurking in between my thoughts. *I'm a pastor. (Some pastor you are.) I'm supposed to have all the answers. (Not sure anyone's going to be looking to you for answers now.) I'm the one who's supposed to have my life together. What would people think? (You know people are talking about you.) Would they still accept me as their pastor?* At times I felt powerless to fight against the condemning thoughts. But the truth is we are not powerless, because once we identify the Shadow Voice, we can silence it by listening to a stronger, better voice.

TURNING TRAGEDY TO TRIUMPH

Years ago, I felt stuck in the middle of my own personal pit of hopelessness and frustration, listening to that Shadow Voice, when I received some much-needed help from an unlikely source. Scott Hamilton is a former Olympic Gold Medalist ice skater and a broadcast commentator for the Winter Olympics. He was well known for his enthusiastic yet excruciating critiques of skaters, with a tenth deduction here and a tenth deduction there. I had known him only as the voice of an expert commentator on a sport I knew little about, but on one particular day I watched a talk show on which he was the featured guest.

During the interview, Hamilton said that everything good in his life came out of devastating circumstances. He fell from the top of the world into a gulf of staggering trials. He suffered through not one, but *two* different battles with cancer. His unexpected message of hope was that your tragedy can also be your triumph. Whether you've lost a loved one, lost your job, or failed in a relationship, these things can be a springboard to take you to a better place. Hamilton explained the difficult place that you are in right now may not be your fault, but it is your responsibility to rise to the challenge. He said you may have a reason to be miserable now, but it's not the events in your life that define you; it's how you deal with them.[2]

I am sure that Hamilton had to wrestle with his own Shadow Voice of fear, self-pity, and hopelessness. He could have caved in to those voices and remained paralyzed in his pain and his past, but he chose a different path. He listened to a higher voice, a stronger voice that gave him the strength and courage to persevere. As I sat there on my couch watching and listening to this interview, wondering what was going to happen next, his words spoke to my heart and gave me the power to make it through the day.

There are many events, circumstances, and struggles in life that are not our fault (though on the other hand, some are definitely our fault!), but regardless of how the trouble started, we have to rise to the occasion to meet the challenge somehow. That day, I made a commitment to myself that my sufferings would not define my life. They might shape my life, but they would not define me. Only God can define me. The ultimate enemy that we battle is not the external challenges, but an internal one. "We wrestle not against flesh and blood, but against principalities, against powers, against the rulers of the darkness of this world" (Ephesians 6:12 KJV). In fact, it's the constant whisper of condemnation, regret, and worry of the Shadow Voice. We must allow a Stronger Voice, God's voice, to silence the Shadow Voice.

One of the ways we allow the Stronger Voice to silence the Shadow Voice is to simply be open. Be open to the wide variety of ways God may be speaking to you. I never expected God to speak to me through a retired ice skater, but He did, and hope was born in my heart that day. God speaks to us through nature. God can speak to us through music. God can speak to us through movies. And God even speaks to us through books. We must be open to the many ways God speaks to us so that we might hear and receive this Stronger Voice. Of course, God will never speak in a way that contradicts Scripture. In fact, later we will look at how His Word is His primary means of communication with us.

Another way we hear the Stronger Voice is through the words of wise friends and counselors. I remember one of my Bible study teachers speaking a profound word to me about how we cannot picture the future without factoring in the grace of God. In other words, when we think about the future, we often project a worst-case scenario where our lives fall apart to the point at which we are broke, sick, and begging on a street corner. We imagine the future without factoring in the grace and provision of God for the trials we may face. I wasn't expecting to hear that Stronger Voice speak to me through this teacher, but I did, and it gave me the courage to face the challenge of the day. Friends and counselors can serve as a reality check when we are going through tough times and traveling down rocky roads. The Shadow Voice can seem so overwhelming and so right that we must seek out the counsel of others to gain perspective and hear that Stronger Voice.

The surest source of the Stronger Voice, God's voice, is His Word. That's why we need to go to church every Sunday to sing the Word of God and to hear the Word of God. We have to read the Word of God, meditate on it, and memorize His Word to allow it to sink deep into our heart and soul. I know this is not easy, especially when your world is unraveling, but that's when we must lean in to God's Word to hear Him speak.

I read Psalm 86 over and over and over again. I stayed there, I lived there daily. Then I started reading the book of Proverbs because I needed wisdom. I read the Proverbs daily, asking God to speak to me so I could receive and live from this place of a Stronger Voice. You can listen to God's Word in your car as you fight traffic. You can listen to God's Word as you take a walk. You can read it first thing in the morning or at the end of a long day. No matter where we are and what we are going through, we need to access the Word of God and allow Him, and His Stronger Voice, to speak to us.

When I was a boy, Cliff Barrows, who served as Billy Graham's worship leader for more than fifty years, was a member of our church. He introduced my father to Dr. Graham and the entire ministry team. One day, I got to tag along with my dad when he went to visit Billy Graham at his home in Montreat, North Carolina. I'll never forget the home-cooked meal of enchiladas Dr. Graham's wife, Ruth, served us and the great time we shared with them. They were both so gracious, so humble, so normal.

NO MATTER WHERE

WE ARE and WHAT WE

ARE GOING THROUGH,

we NEED TO ACCESS

the WORD OF GOD

and ALLOW HIM, and

HIS STRONGER VOICE,

TO SPEAK TO US.

Before we left, Billy asked my dad to read the Bible to him, which was so surprising. I would've expected him to read it to us! So my dad picked up the Bible, found a passage, and read it out loud to me and Dr. Graham as we sat in his den. I thought this request was unique to us, but through the years I read other accounts of people who had visited him in his home, saying he did the exact same thing—asked them to read Scripture to him. Even Billy Graham needed someone else to speak the Word to him. He needed to hear the Stronger Voice of God speak to him in that moment, in that day, to make it through.

The continual challenge we face is to allow the Stronger Voice to silence the Shadow Voice, to live from God's place of strength and courage rather than from the place of shame, regret, and self-pity. The Shadow Voice tempts us to give up, live in the pain of the past, and not continue our journey forward. You must be open to how God speaks to you in his Stronger Voice—through wise counsel, through the Word, and through worship. This will help you continue to survive today and move toward a place where you are thriving. It helps you transition from the place of disorientation to reorientation.

But how do we do that? How do we stay open to God's voice and follow what He's telling us to do? Dealing with this Shadow Voice is so critical to surviving the day that I devoted another chapter in this book to dive deeper into how we can combat it. (See chapter 10.) But first, in order to keep moving forward in our lives, we need to look at three choices we must make as we navigate crisis and loss. During my darkest days, I chose to embrace humility, grace, and surrender. Sometimes I wonder if I chose them or they chose me, but regardless, these choices were game changers for me, and they can be for you too. Not only are they beneficial, but they're powerful positions we all can take. Yes, we all know about these concepts, but making them an integral part of who we are is different from knowing about them. Allow me to unpack each one of them in the next section, part 2, and show you how advantageous they can be regardless of your circumstances.

SURVIVAL PRAYER:

Father, the Shadow Voice speaks lies into my heart every day, and I don't feel I can escape it. I know You are the Stronger Voice I must hear in this moment. I choose to discard the lies of the Shadow Voice and listen to the truth of Your Stronger Voice. Help me to receive and be empowered by Your voice as I walk through this day with You.

SURVIVAL PASSAGE:

> My sheep listen to my voice; I know them, and
> they follow me.

John 10:27

SURVIVAL PRACTICE:

Memorize a short phrase from God's Word that you repeat to yourself over and over again as you walk through this day. For example, you could repeat this phrase: "The LORD is my Shepherd; I shall not want" (Psalm 23:1 KJV).

PART TWO

THE CHOICE TO MOVE FORWARD

CHAPTER FIVE

WHEN THE PAIN REMAINS

"We cannot choose our external circumstances, but we can always choose how we respond to them."

Epictetus

When I was a boy, my father bought my brother and me a yellow lawn mower. Just about every Saturday we pushed that cheap piece of tin back and forth to cut what seemed to be a plot of grass the size of a football field. When our family later moved to Houston in the late '70s, my brother and I stopped mowing our lawn. We were too busy playing basketball, chasing girls, and trying to graduate from high school to worry about the yard.

However, years later when I got out of school, I rented an old duplex with a backyard that felt as if it were the size of the state of California. When the grass grew to be fifteen feet high, I decided it was time to come out of my yard-maintenance retirement plan.

I borrowed a mower from my uncle, who lived around the corner, and pushed that heavy green Lawn-Boy all over the yard until the task was complete. There's nothing like the smell of fresh-cut grass.

Now I had a routine. Every two weeks I would walk over to my uncle's house, borrow the Lawn-Boy, mow my grass, and return the mower. On one super-humid Houston Saturday, I found myself once again sweating, pushing, and pulling the Green Monster all over my yard. Then *it* happened. While I was attempting a U-turn, my hand slipped on the handlebars and seemingly bent the thing in two. I panicked because I thought I had broken my uncle's lawn mower, and then, whoa …

Suddenly the lawn mower took off by itself as if it had a mind of its own. Once I realized what had happened, I felt like an idiot. Since I had not mowed a lawn in more than a decade, I was clueless about the newfangled, self-propelled gems. I had exerted all of my strength and effort, gritting my teeth, sweat pouring down from my face like a waterfall, when all I had to do was guide the mower with my fingertips and let it do all the work. The power was always there; I was just clueless about how to access it.

For so long I tried to live by my own effort and willpower. I sweated and toiled daily to love the people I worked with, to stop a nagging habit, or to resist a temptation that constantly knocked at my door. I thought it was my responsibility to fix and control everything that was spiraling out of control in my life. I lived as if I had to do all the work and forgot about the power that God had placed inside me. Finally, the pain and chaos of my own life shouted to me the absolute necessity of trusting in God's empowering grace.

There were reasons I had my therapist on speed dial several years ago and for my *What about Bob?* fits on the floor. It's complicated, but the bottom line is that my life was falling apart. After years of struggle, months of therapy, tears, prayers, and help from others, my nineteen-year marriage ended in divorce. I felt like an utter failure. Prior to this, I never could have dreamed of getting a divorce. It was more plausible that I would deny Christ and become an atheist or fly to Mars and become a Martian than end up divorced. And yet, my marriage ended in a heartbreaking divorce.

Divorce is devastating and destructive in so many ways. It virtually rips the heart and soul out of your body, your family, your friends, and your precious children. I cringe when someone says, "They're going through a brutal divorce," as if there was such a thing as a non-brutal divorce. But this was my brutal divorce. The circumstances were beyond my control, but I still felt like I had thoroughly let down my kids, my parents, and the church I served. A legion of lies and rumors swirled around me about affairs with women and men. These slanderous words rained down on my family and me for years. It was only by the power of God and a few trusted friends that I made it through that dark, devastating season. My excruciating life storm thrust me onto the floor, crying out to God. It was a beatdown that forced me into a position of humility and humiliation like I'd never experienced before.

FAILURES,

DISAPPOINTMENTS,

and **SUFFERING** are

NOT ONLY COMMON,

THEY'RE also a **SURE**

PATH to **HUMILITY**.

I pray you never have to experience that kind of pain or failure in your life. But the truth is that failures, disappointments, and suffering are not only common, they're also a sure path to humility. We live in a broken, fallen world with broken, fallen people who do broken, fallen things. I do broken, fallen things. You do broken, fallen things. Multiply that brokenness and fallenness by eight billion people and you have a massive, incalculable amount of pain and heartache that can have a powerful, humbling effect on us.

Our ability to survive the world of hurt we live in will depend on the next steps we make. In order to move forward into a new tomorrow, we must make some wise choices to be empowered by God. Many times in our lives it's the pain and pressure of life storms that push us into God's presence and give us the opportunity to make these vital choices. First, we must choose humility and understand who God is and who we are in light of Him. God is our maker and the one who designed us to live in a trusting relationship with Him. Humility is all about being down to earth, grateful, and open to the help God is sending our way. The second choice is to receive God's radical acceptance that flows to us through Jesus Christ. God's grace covers us and tells us that we are forgiven, accepted, and loved by Him.

Every day I must choose to live my life before God on the basis of grace. Without His grace, I am powerless over my humanity and my ongoing painful circumstances. Why? Because grace is not only about God's radical acceptance of us through Christ; it's also about the power He provides to sustain us and give us strength.

POWER IN WEAKNESS

Though he passed away the year I was born, C. S. Lewis impacted my life in a profound way. It would be impossible to quantify his influence on me. Not long ago, Academy Award winner Anthony Hopkins portrayed the life of the Oxford professor and prolific writer in one of my favorite movies, *Shadowlands*, a gripping story about Lewis's awakening to the harsh realities of passionate love and the nature of suffering. The weight of surviving the day was bearing down hard on Lewis.

In one scene, as his wife is dying of cancer, a well-meaning colleague from Oxford encourages him to pray for her recovery. Lewis chides him with his classic response, "I pray because I can't help myself; I pray because I'm helpless. I pray because the need flows out of me all the time, waking and sleeping. It doesn't change God; it changes me."[1] In other words, this great man of the faith wasn't praying because he suddenly found himself in crisis. He was always in prayer anyway, and he understood that his primary motivation for prayer was not to manipulate God, but to bring about a transformation in his own heart. He needed God's empowering grace to make it through the day, to encourage him and give him the strength to carry on.

Prayer isn't a hocus-pocus process whereby we say magic words with enough faith in order for God to grant our wish. On the contrary, prayer is an ongoing process of communication that enables us to become more like Christ and to discover God's desires for our lives. That's not to say that our prayers don't have an impact on us, our circumstances, or others. We are in joint cooperation with God as the agents of change in the world around us. But prayer is ultimately about changing our hearts. Prayer is about receiving the empowering grace of God each day.

In 2 Corinthians 12, Paul was pleading with God to remove a mysterious "thorn in the flesh" causing him much pain and difficulty. Paul prayed to God three times to remove his thorn. How many times have you asked God to remove you from a tough situation or take away some excruciating pain? I can't count the number of times I have.

Paul had this thorn in the flesh. It was painful, chronic, either a physical illness or circumstance. We don't know exactly what it was. What did he do about it? Look at verse 8. Paul said, "Three times I pleaded with the Lord to take it away from me." Time and time again he shouted out, "God, take it away. God, take it away. Lord, take it away." The response? Silence. Paul screamed out to a deaf heaven, "Take it away!" And nothing happened. I'm not talking about myself here. I'm talking about Paul, the apostle Paul. The guy who experienced the supernatural power of answered prayer like we may never know in our lifetime.

Read through Acts chapter 13 all the way to Acts 28 and count the miracles that were performed and the prayers that were answered at Paul's very hands. Those who were crippled could suddenly walk. People simply touched his handkerchief and they were healed. He even raised someone from the dead. Powerful stuff! And if anyone could have earned God's mercy, it was Paul. He risked his life. He was beaten. He was whipped. He was imprisoned. He was shipwrecked. And he still served God. Crying out to God, not for his own comfort, but so he could continue to do God's will. "Take it away. God, take it away. Lord, change these circumstances."

God said, "No. I'm not going to take it away." For fourteen years, Paul must have heard "No. These painful circumstances are not going to change. They're not going to change. You must learn to accept them. I'm not going to intervene this time. You've got to radically accept this thorn." So is that the end of the story? Is this the end of Paul? What does God tell Paul?

Paul wrote, "He said to me, 'My grace is sufficient for you, for my power is made perfect in weakness.' Therefore, I will boast all the more gladly about my weaknesses, so that Christ's power may rest on me" (2 Corinthians 12:9). In other words, God said, "You have to accept your thorn. It's always going to be there, but I will give you the empowering grace to make it through. And in your pain, and in your weakness, and in this thorn, people will see My power working through you." This is the empowering grace of God.

We all have our painful thorns that will not go away. I think about my friend who is quadriplegic, my other friend who struggles with Parkinson's disease, one friend whose special-needs child is twenty-one years old in diapers and has never spoken a word. These are harsh, painful circumstances that will not change for the better but in most cases will continue to get worse. They have radically accepted these circumstances and survived them with great courage and even joy. The depth of their lives is so profound and authentic.

Whatever your thorn is, God may be saying to you, "Listen, I have all the grace you need for this." When you stand in radical acceptance, like Paul did, God will give you the empowering grace to handle your circumstances. Then watch as His power is manifested in your life.

GOD'S NO IS ALSO HIS YES

When God says no to removing our thorns, He simultaneously says yes to His grace. God provides the grace, the power to stand, the power to fight, the power to make it through the day when we need it. I wish it were the opposite. I wish He were in the thorn-removal business instead of the thorn-management business, but that's not always how it is. But take heart, because God's no is also His yes.

Perhaps you have a weakness in your life that you want God to remove. Maybe it's a tough family life, an emotional wound from the past, chronic physical pain, ridicule from people who don't understand your faith, or the stress of making it through a hectic week at work. God will not always pull you out of a stressful scenario or miraculously zap the pain from your body, but He does promise to give you sufficient grace for the need of the moment. He promises to say yes when you need grace.

We never get away from God's empowering, supernatural, sustaining grace. It's that overwhelming, never-ending, reckless love and grace of God that empowers us despite our thorns and our circumstances. But we also have to do something with our thorns. According to Hebrews 4:16, "Let us then with confidence draw near to the throne of grace, that we may receive mercy and find grace to help in time of need" (ESV). In other words, take your thorn to the throne. Take your painful circumstances, your difficult situation, that may never change, and go straight to the throne of grace. There God will give you the mercy you need.

British theologian John Blanchard said, "Listen, for daily needs, there's daily grace. For sudden needs, there's sudden grace. For overwhelming need, there will be overwhelming grace."[2] But we have a responsibility to daily, sometimes hourly, take our thorn to the throne and say, "God, I need Your grace right now, in this moment." Sometimes you have to push yourself into God's presence. "God, I'm dealing with this hellacious thorn again. It's me again. Lord, I need Your grace today." He will always respond with the grace for it. Take your thorn to the throne even when it seems like prayer isn't working.

He may not change your circumstances, but He will change you. He will fill you with the grace and power to make it through this day. Not tomorrow (yet). Today. When you are weak, His strength can make you strong.

A DAILY INVITATION

Check out what Matthew wrote down as he remembered the words of the Messiah. Jesus offered, "Come to me, all you who are weary and burdened, and I will give you rest. Take my yoke upon you and learn from me, for I am gentle and humble in heart, and you will find rest for your souls. For my yoke is easy and my burden is light" (Matthew 11:28–30). What a wonderful invitation. Jesus invites us to come to Him for new life.

His offer is continuous because we are always in need of a fresh supply of His grace to lift our burdens, to remind us that our burdens have already been lifted. We need a fresh supply of His perspective on our lives, our schedules, on the worries and anxieties and pressures of life. We need His strength to make it through the day, to make it through the week. It's a daily invitation to come to Him.

If we could extend a microphone to heaven and interview Paul about how he was able to endure ridicule, persecution, beatings, imprisonments, and ultimately face his death, he would most likely say, "I stayed focused on grace." He penned the words "Be strong in the grace that is in Christ Jesus" to his young disciple Timothy shortly before his martyrdom in Rome (2 Timothy 2:1); he was pleading with this future leader, "If you want your life to have maximum impact, if you truly want to make a difference for God in this brief stay here on earth, then focus like a laser on the grace of God."

For the past fourteen years, God has been opening my eyes to His amazing grace. And I guarantee you that if you will focus on grace, your life will continue to change, and your relationships will be enhanced. Grace will change the way you experience God. Grace will give you compassion toward other people. Grace will change the way you see yourself. It will take you off the performance treadmill and free you up to walk in the love and acceptance of God through Jesus Christ.

The Message phrases Matthew 11:28–30 like this, "Are you tired? Worn out? Burned out on religion? Come to me. Get away with me and you'll recover your life. I'll show you how to take a real rest. Walk with me and work with me—watch how I do it. Learn the unforced rhythms of grace. I won't lay anything heavy or ill-fitting on you. Keep company with me and you'll learn to live freely and lightly." God meets us in the midst of our pain. He can redeem our past and lead us into a better future. He is with us in the daily pressures of life as we cast that burden on Him.

GRACE FOR ONE DAY AT A TIME

I've never met anyone in my life who's lived out the incredible, daily empowering of God's grace more than Corrie ten Boom, a survivor of a Nazi concentration camp. When I was a young boy, Corrie spoke at our church and then came to our house for lunch. Someone once asked her how she was able to survive the horrors and torments of Hitler's death camp, and here is how she responded: "When I was a little girl growing up in Holland, the train was a primary means of transportation. If I had to take a trip to Amsterdam, my father would buy my ticket weeks in advance. However, he would not give me the ticket until the day of my journey, for fear that I might lose it."[3] She explained how God did the same thing for her while she was in prison. He gave her just enough strength, just enough grace, for that particular day and that particular challenge.

Likewise, when the Israelites were stuck in the desert thousands of years ago, God rained down manna from heaven for their daily bread. They could not save the manna for the future or it would spoil, so they had to remain dependent on God's daily supply.

It's wonderful to know that the same God who provided food for the Israelites in the desert and courage for Corrie ten Boom in prison provides for you and me as well. As you look to the future and try to forecast all the trials and sufferings you may experience in this life, it's easy to become overwhelmed. Where will you find the strength to endure? How will you face the pain? How will you know what to do? The following chapters lay out some essential choices that will help you access this grace day by day by day. For now, let's take a deep breath and breathe in God's grace. Remember, God promises daily grace to you—one day at a time. When you are weak, He is strong. Pray that His power will shine through your weakness. Don't worry about tomorrow's journey. He will give you the ticket of grace when you need it.

SURVIVAL PRAYER:

Father, I trust in Your power and strength to make it through the day. When I am faced with problems and circumstances too difficult to bear, I choose to lean on Your power to enable me to make it through.

SURVIVAL PASSAGE:

> Therefore, in order to keep me from becoming conceited, I was given a thorn in my flesh, a messenger of Satan, to torment me. Three times I pleaded with the Lord to take it away from me.

But he said to me, "My grace is sufficient for you, for my power is made perfect in weakness." Therefore I will boast all the more gladly about my weaknesses, so that Christ's power may rest on me. That is why, for Christ's sake, I delight in weaknesses, in insults, in hardships, in persecutions, in difficulties. For when I am weak, then I am strong.

2 Corinthians 12:7–10

SURVIVAL PRACTICE:

Write down what your thorn is, and ask God to give you the power today to deal with your thorn.

CHAPTER SIX

CHOOSING GOD'S JIU-JITSU

"I think human beings have a moral obligation to pursue humility as a trait. We are better people when we are humble. It's easier to learn. It's easier to get along with others. It's easier to appreciate the world around you."
Malcolm Gladwell

While most people are throwing down Chinese food or picking up their dry cleaning in the middle of the day, I am getting beat up, bruised, and bloodied by complete strangers and some well-meaning friends. Choking and getting choked. Breaking an arm and getting my arm broken. Dislocating a shoulder and getting my shoulder dislocated. Smashing and getting smashed. Okay, no one is really getting mortally injured during my lunch hour, but we come pretty close. No, I am not auditioning for *Fight Club Part Two*; I'm merely learning the art of Brazilian jiu-jitsu (known as BJJ).

I started training years ago in order to learn how to defend myself and as a "gentle" symbolic reminder that life is a fight. One of the lessons I gleaned early on from my instructors was the importance of always being in the right position. They call it "position before submission"—you have to be in the right position before you can submit (beat) your opponent. Jiu-jitsu is not about using strength to out-muscle your opponent. It is about leverage. Getting in position so you can have the advantage, even against a bigger, stronger opponent. You want to use the strong, heavy part of your body against the weaker part of your opponent's body. You want to wrap both of your arms around the other guy's neck, because your two arms are stronger than his Adam's apple and carotid arteries. In other words, you must be in the right position—a dominant, controlling position—before you can attack your opponent to submit him. Submitting someone is getting him to tap out or give up, which is like saying "Uncle" or "Okay, I quit."

So for months on end, I practiced position after position after position. I stopped caring about winning or losing. I just wanted to be in the right position. With this new mind-set, my chances of winning a match increased dramatically. Much more than if I had not mastered the concept of positioning. For me, BJJ has been great physical training, but so many of the principles have also been helpful more broadly in my life.

In BJJ terms, you could say my life had gotten to the point where I needed to tap out. My world was collapsing all around me. When I entered into the world of divorce, shared custody, and single parenting, I did not know how I would make it through. The shame and guilt of the *D* word weighed heavily upon me. God hates divorce. I hate divorce. I preached and wrote books against divorce. I led seminars around the country to help prevent divorce, and now it was happening to my family. Fear, dread, and shame flooded my heart every morning for years. The emotional battle threatened to overwhelm every aspect of my life. I felt so afraid and so alone.

Everything in my life was changing. I didn't know if I would have to change careers. I thought that my life in ministry was certainly over. I contemplated going to law school, becoming a teacher, or pursuing a degree in counseling. I had no idea what my job would be after this storm passed. I was trying to control everything on my own. I had to figure out next steps. I had to wrap my head around how parenting my children would change. I worried about what people thought of me. I was working on my eulogy for my career as a pastor. I finally reached my breaking point (cue the crying on my therapist's floor). Done. Tap.

And then, in God's infinite mercy, when I finally surrendered, He reminded me of my dependence on Him. That I *can* depend on Him. That I *must* depend on Him. I had reached the end of myself. At this point tapping out of thinking I was the solution to my current predicament was becoming more appealing. All my best efforts could not fix my life. I started to give up depending on myself and was learning in a fresh way to reposition myself under God with Him in His rightful place. All it took was … humility.

WHAT IS HUMILITY?

Clinical psychologist Jordan Peterson defines *humility* as the "recognition of personal insufficiency and the willingness to learn."[1] Check. I was definitely insufficient to put the million little pieces of my life back together and move forward. Therefore, I needed to be willing to learn. Check. To be humble and to cultivate humility is to recognize who God is, and who we are in light of who He is. We realize that God is great and we are not. He is transcendent and we are finite and limited in comparison. Humility is seeing our flawed, selfish, sinful humanity in light of His blameless, perfect, and holy character. Humility is the daily awareness of our dependency on God and responding with appropriate trust and obedience.

HOW DO WE BEGIN TO POSITION OURSELVES WITH HUMILITY?

Humility starts with the realization that we are not omniscient or omnipotent and that God almighty is. A good start is to begin the day by stating the truth of who He is and who we are until we actually believe it. Try something like, "God, You are the Creator and I am the created. You formed the world. I just live in it. You see and know everything, and I see and know so very little. You know all that will happen today and in the future; therefore, You know what I need today and tomorrow. I know I need You to guide me through each and every day." Starting our day with a prayer like that puts us in a position of humility where we can allow God the space to work in our lives. It reminds us that we are to be faithful but that God is ultimately in control. Isaiah 55:8–9 puts our relational position with God in perspective so well. "'For my thoughts are not your thoughts, neither are your ways my ways,' declares the LORD. 'As the heavens are higher than the earth, so are my ways higher than your ways and my thoughts than your thoughts.'" Beginning my day in a position of humility has connected me with God on a deeper level. It has helped me be more open to receiving His peace, His wisdom, and His guidance.

HOW DO WE KNOW WE ARE IN THE RIGHT POSITION?

As I began to humble myself before Him in recognition that He was the King of the universe (all of it, including my chaotic upside-down world) and conversely that I was not, over time, I slowly started to breathe again. My circumstances hadn't changed. But I was no longer bearing the full weight of my world anymore. I no longer saw myself as uniquely necessary to keep all the plates spinning and the whole world turning. Gradually, I stopped seeing myself as the sole caretaker of my family. He was with me. And He was ultimately in control (the whole part of "being a sovereign God" thing). In time I became more admittedly dependent on Him and more connected to Him than I ever imagined. The truth of who God was certainly was not new to me. (I am a pastor with three degrees.) But living in the light of this truth and having to lean into it on a daily basis to keep my sanity was a process that I had to adjust to and practice.

HUMILITY IS A DAILY PRACTICE WE NEVER OUTGROW

Imagine a two-year-old declaring his autonomy and saying, "Mom, Dad, I am leaving the house and doing things on my own now. I've got my sippy cup and blankie packed. I'm out of here!" Ridiculous. He cannot survive out on his own. He doesn't have the capacity to do that yet. Like all babies, he's dependent in so many ways. And as God's children, we are as well. Yet we forget that and in the same way we go about our lives as if we have outgrown the God who created us and longs to lead us and guide us down our uncertain path.

We never outgrow our dependency on God, and we never outgrow our position with God. We were created by God and for God. We are dependent on Him for our very existence. Understanding this brings perspective. This is who God is; this is who I am. I need to listen to God and live the way He desires for me to live in this moment, in this day.

Our only reasonable response to the God who created us is to bow down in awesome wonder. This is the first and foremost choice we must make. This is the only right position for us to take before God in order to relate to Him, receive from Him, and follow Him. We must be connected to the Source of Life in order to make sense out of life and survive this day. Humility helps us survive the day in many ways.

HUMILITY helps us

SURVIVE THE DAY

in MANY WAYS.

HUMILITY POSITIONS US TO START THE HEALING PROCESS

About two decades ago, my good friend Mark walked into a meeting and admitted that he was powerless over alcohol and that his life had become unmanageable. He did not believe in God (yet) but had the courage and humility to admit defeat. That confession, that small dose of humility, led to freedom and a new life beyond his dreams.

The meeting he went to was held by Alcoholics Anonymous (AA), indisputably the most successful program for delivering people from substance abuse and other addictions. The Twelve Steps Program is foundational to AA. And the first and most critical step is to admit that we're powerless over alcohol and that our lives have become unmanageable. It is another way of admitting we are spiritually poor, helpless, and at the end of our ropes. Whatever our vice is—alcohol, drugs, pride, fill in the blank—we must acknowledge that we do not have power over it, and that our life is out of our control. That's the first step to healing and sanity, a step that's all about humility.

The Bible puts it this way: "God opposes the proud but gives grace to the humble" (1 Peter 5:5 ESV). I strongly believe humility is essential to make it through the most difficult times in this life.

HUMILITY POSITIONS US TO REACH OUT

So often in life, we can't do it all on our own and we need the help of others. God created us to live in community. In Genesis, God said it was not good for man to be alone. We aren't supposed to be 100 percent self-sufficient. We need each other. In the cycle of life, we start out as dependent infants, grow to be productive adults, and then grow old and become dependent again. So giving and accepting help are part of our natural cycle of life. This is more broadly true in all of life—we are continually and variably giving and receiving help in many different ways. But as adults, sometimes admitting we need help can be humbling, and painfully so.

Every day I acknowledge who God is and who I am. I set my will to stay dependent on God, to be open to receive help from God, help from others, and also to be committed to serving others. This is the way of humility.

HUMILITY POSITIONS US TO SERVE

Jesus was the ultimate example of servant leadership. He modeled how we are to serve those closest to us as well as serve beyond our own circle of family and friends. Jesus washed His own disciples' feet, but then He also fed the 5,000. If the God of the universe came down to save us and serve us, then we are to follow His lead and serve too. The social media world entices us to care all about ourselves and the shallower things in life (e.g., how we look) and to compare ourselves to others. Quietly serving your elderly neighbor is the silent rebellion that is needed to bring kindness, generosity, and thoughtfulness to an increasingly preoccupied world. Get involved in anything your church is doing to serve those who are less fortunate in your city.

My best friend, Dave, who is so darn practical and wise, said it this way, "The world would be such a better place if everyone would just shut up and serve." That's so true. Even when we are barely making it through the day, when we "shut up and serve" others, we are practicing humility. And serving connects us to our mutual humanity with everyone else on the planet. We're not special, different, or better; we are just all trying to figure out this thing called life. And when we do that, it also helps us get outside of our heads and our own small worlds and look around. Sometimes getting out and entering into the world of others is the best prescription for what ails our own! Looking outward can be a great relief to gazing inward!

HUMILITY POSITIONS US TO BE GRATEFUL

I have a friend who was raised in a single-parent family in a dirt-poor country. Against the odds, he rose above his circumstances, got a degree, and became a highly successful businessman. One day, gripped by worry and anxiety, he came home from work with the weight of the world on his shoulders. He told his wife how burdened he was, and their housekeeper overheard the conversation. She quietly approached him and said, "Mr. Allen, may I tell you what I do when I feel this way? I get down on my knees and start to thank God for everything I can think of. And by the time I get off my knees, my worries are gone."

I like that. Though it's a counterintuitive action, it's one of the most powerful choices we can make in the face of adversity. Humility reminds me to kneel before God in gratitude and also to kneel before others. When I feel overwhelmed by life, when the problems creep in, when I begin to wonder what God is doing or not doing, I get down on my knees and start thanking Him. I thank Him for the bed I slept on. I thank Him for my cup of morning coffee. I thank Him that I have a job. I thank Him for my health, for my family, for a roof over my head. Staying thankful—and getting specific about it—helps me.

WHAT HUMILITY IS NOT

It must be emphasized that humility is not walking around moping and feeling down with no self-esteem. And it's not a contest to see who can be the most humble and lowly. I like the more modern definition of *humility*, which says humility is not thinking less of yourself, it's thinking of yourself less. Rather than viewing yourself as lowly and unworthy, it's knowing who you are, what you're worth, what you're capable of, but having no need to prove anything to anyone else. After all, we are worth the life of God's only Son, aren't we? Humility is quiet strength. When we are humble, we own the identity, strengths, and talents God has given us and use them to serve others. It's realizing that everything we have is a gift from God, even our ability to work hard and improve in different areas of life. When we take our eyes off of ourselves (in pride) and others (in comparison) and focus on Him and all He has provided, we find peace and love.

HUMILITY IS NOT

THINKING LESS

of yourself.

IT'S thinking

of YOURSELF LESS.

THE POSITION PRINCIPLE

Over the many years of my jiu-jitsu training, I've grappled with world-class black belts, mixed martial arts (MMA) cage fighters, struggling beginners, and everyone in between. Many times I've ask my training partners or professors what they have learned from engaging in this practice. To a person, they will say humility. Nothing humbles you more than when a smaller, physically weaker opponent dominates you and makes you tap (give up). It's amazing and humbling. How does the underdog submit and defeat the giant? Back to the all-important position principle: position before submission.

When life's storms come, they can knock us down and tempt us to tap out. But we can find strength and stability when we are in a position of humility and aware of our dependency on God. How do we defeat the giants and survive the storms in our lives and move forward and survive the day? Position ourselves in a place of humility.

When we start on our knees, we align our hearts and minds in such a way that we hear the Stronger Voice of God and are empowered to live it out in the context of our lives. We have to be in the right position before God and others to triumph in our personal jiu-jitsu matches—the daily trials and battles we face.

SURVIVAL PRAYER:

God, I choose to humble myself before You today. You are God, and I am not. I am desperate for You to be my rock today. Use all of my talents, my gifts, my failure, my pain to be of service to someone else. I will look for others to serve throughout this day.

SURVIVAL PASSAGE:

All of you, clothe yourselves with humility toward one another, because,

"God opposes the proud
but shows favor to the humble."

Humble yourselves, therefore, under God's mighty hand, that he may lift you up in due time. Cast all your anxiety on him because he cares for you.

1 Peter 5:5–7

SURVIVAL PRACTICE:

Put in your calendar three ways you can help someone else today.

CHAPTER SEVEN

UNEXPECTED LOVE

*"Our worst days are never so bad that we are beyond
the reach of God's grace. Our best days are never so
good that we are beyond the need of God's grace."*

Jerry Bridges

My mom passed away a few years ago after a long battle with a rare autoimmune disease. She had been in and out of hospitals for four years. About three months before she passed, I went up to the hospital to visit her. She was watching yet another episode of *Fixer Upper* with Chip and Joanna Gaines. The hospital room was very quiet, and my mom couldn't talk because she was on life support with a ventilator in her throat, but sometimes she could mouth some words. By that time, I had learned how to read her lips somewhat. We were sitting there "talking" in our adapted way when my mom stopped, looked around, lifted her left hand, then pointed at something across the room. I could tell that she wanted me to bring her something. I stood up and tried to figure out what she wanted.

"Is that what you want?" I picked up a picture of her beloved dog, Winston. "Is this it? Is this what you were pointing at?" She shook her head. So I picked up a notepad with a pen on top of it. Yes. She reached for it. My mom was an artist and in earlier days had beautiful handwriting, but at this stage her hands were shaking as she labored to write something down. I stepped over to her bedside and read the three words she had painstakingly scribbled out: "I love you." She wanted to be sure I knew, in case there was any doubt, that she loved me.

My mom, who for over fifty years observed all my faults, all my failures, all my pain, loved me. Even though she struggled to get her next breath, she wanted me, her son, to know that she loved me. I knew my mom loved me, but her expression of love at that moment caught me off guard. It was unexpected.

To know that we are deeply loved by another human being is healing. But to know that we are loved by the God of the universe fills us with a power and gratitude that is life changing. There's another name for God's unexpected love for us. It's called grace. And grace is what we need when we don't feel so loved and accepted as we journey through this life storm.

When my daughter was young, I taught her to ride a bike without training wheels. She would fall over time and time again like we all did. I told her, "Angel, half of life is simply getting back up when you fall down." But sometimes life hits us so hard we don't know if we can get back up. Sometimes when we're down, it feels like a weight is on top of us, holding us down to the ground. When life hits us smack between the eyes, we wonder if we can get up. Then we finally do get up, only to be knocked down again.

We may think, *Should I even try to get back up?* Then we start looking at our lives, our families, our loved ones, our friends, our finances. We begin to ask hard questions. *Did I do something wrong here? Am I being punished? Is this why I can't make it through the day? How will I ever get through this? Will my life ever get better?* The weight of those questions can feel crushing to our souls.

Living with our past and dealing with real, overwhelming pain and pressure is kind of like carrying around a huge, heavy weight on our backs. And sometimes life gets so crazy and confusing that our burdens seem too heavy to bear. When I was in the midst of my own battle, I asked myself, *Where is God in all of this? If God loves me, how can I practically receive that grace every day when I feel so unlovable and unforgivable?*

It helps me to turn to the Bible and read the stories of men and women who felt just like I did—unlovable, unforgivable, carrying around this heavy weight. I try to read their stories not like they are some super saint, but like they are everyday people just trying to make it through the day and follow God through their own life storms. Luckily, the Bible doesn't give us photoshopped, cleaned-up, Instagram images of perfect people. Thankfully, it gives us the freedom to ask those searching questions. It gives us the real and the raw. The good, the bad, and the unusual. I relate to it because my own story includes those elements. They're certainly evident in Peter's story as well.

Peter failed. With great passion he told Jesus he would never deny Him, but he would sooner die for Him. But rather than offering His heartfelt thanks for the pledge of Peter's dying loyalty, Jesus called him out: "The truth is that before the rooster crows, you'll deny me three times" (John 13:37–38 THE MESSAGE). Fast-forward through the story, and Jesus was arrested and put on trial. Peter sat warming himself by the fire. Just as Jesus had predicted, Peter denied Him three times. Three times. To be sure people believed him, he insisted, "I don't know the man." Brutal. He failed, and he may as well have had a big *F* tattooed on his chest. There was no plus sign to be found.

Peter must have lived in a heavy fog of guilt, shame, and fear all day Friday, all day Saturday, and all day Sunday. The Shadow Voice must have weighed heavily upon him for those three long days. But then, risen from the tomb, Jesus appeared to him. And three times Jesus said to Peter, "Feed my sheep. Feed my sheep. Feed my sheep" (see John 21). Jesus was offering him absolution for all three denials with three grace-filled propositions to counter his three failures. Peter the Boldest had become Peter the Broken. But now, Peter the Broken was again Peter the Boldest. Bold because of his own pride? No, bold because in humility he received the grace of God.

Later, Peter wrote, "Clothe yourselves, all of you, with humility toward one another, for 'God opposes the proud but gives grace to the humble.' Humble yourselves, therefore, under the mighty hand of God so that at the proper time he may exalt you, casting all your anxieties on him, because he cares for you" (1 Peter 5:5–7 ESV). Did you catch that? God gives grace to the humble. Even though Peter wrote these encouraging words many, many years ago, they still provide strength to those of us who are enduring much pain and pressure today.

As we saw in the previous chapter, boldness begins when we get into the right position of humility before God. Humility brings us to the realization of our desperate need for God and of our need to align our will with His will. Humility is God's ground zero. It puts us in the place to open up to God's help and enables us to do what He tells us to do.

Remember, the first choice you must make to survive the day is to *humble yourself* before God and others. This first choice puts us in the right position for the second choice, which is to *receive God's grace*. God's multifaceted grace opens our hearts to God's forgiveness, His acceptance, and His love.

THE MOST POWERFUL FORCE IN THE UNIVERSE

When I was a little boy growing up in the South, whenever I would eat at a friend's house for supper, the mom would ask, "Who's gonna say grace?" It's an interesting phrase, "Say grace." What does it mean? The practical answer is that it means to pray over the food. When I lived in Mexico City, before every meal, the father of the house would say, "*Vamos orar hermanos.*" I was still learning Spanish, so I didn't know what that phrase meant at the time, but the next thing I knew, everyone at the table would bow their heads to pray. Later I learned that the phrase means "We are going to pray, brothers." In other words, bow your heads because we are about to "say grace."

I "said grace" at mealtimes for many years before I ever knew the depths, the simplicity, and the power of grace. To survive the day, this difficult day, we need grace. The choice we face on a daily basis is to open our hearts to the grace God gives us. His super-abounding, inexhaustible, replenishing grace. Like so many Christians, I "said grace" before I understood it, felt it, and chose to live in it. When every means of escape seems like a door slammed in your face, grace comes along and opens new doors. Grace is what we need in this present moment.

In his book *Addiction and Grace*, Gerald May addressed the absolute necessity for receiving this transcendent spiritual power called grace. "Understanding will not deliver us from addiction, but it will, I hope, help us appreciate grace. Grace is the most powerful force in the universe. It can transcend repression, addiction and every other internal and external power that seeks to oppress the freedom of the human heart. Grace is where our hope lies."[1]

Grace is not only for those struggling with addiction; it's also for those struggling to make sense of life and endure hard times. Sometimes we need this most powerful force in the universe in order to survive one more day.

THE ONLY WAY TO DEAL WITH OUR PAST

Jesus told the story of two men who went up to church to pray. One man was religious (perhaps a Baptist); the other man was irreligious (perhaps a bar owner). The Baptist said, "Lord, I am so glad that I go to church, read Your Word, and vote the right way. I'm so proud that I am humble and not like that wretched sinner over there." The bar owner would not even look up but bowed his head and muttered the words, "Lord, have mercy on me, a sinner." Then Jesus asked, "Which one do you think went home justified?" In other words, which one was accepted and forgiven by God? Which one would receive God's grace? Obviously, the lowly bar owner. Jesus said, "I tell you that this man, rather than the other, went home justified before God. For all those who exalt themselves will be humbled, and those who humble themselves will be exalted" (see Luke 18).

And there it is again. The connection between humility and grace. In the words of James, the brother of Jesus, "But he gives us more grace. That is why Scripture says: 'God opposes the proud but shows favor to the humble'" (James 4:6).

Sometimes only God can orchestrate the kind of revelation in which we wake up to the knowledge that He is big, powerful, and holy—and we are not. When we realize that we are just mud and clay, and we finally see our spiritual poverty before Him, we realize there is nothing we can do to make ourselves right. We can't climb out of the hole by ourselves. We can't climb the ladder of good works and clean up our act enough to earn His grace. He's going to have to do it for us.

The best way to deal with our past is through the grace of God. In fact, the *only* way to deal with our past is through the grace of God. Grace is not only receiving what we do not deserve; it's also receiving the opposite of what we deserve. The only way we can move forward and take on this day is to choose to receive God's grace. No one is good enough. No one has figured out the path to perfection. The good news is God uses people like you and me to make a difference just like He did with the sinner-saints we study in the Bible.

Paul persecuted and executed Christians before the grace of God appeared and the most powerful force in the universe transformed him into a follower of the Christ he once persecuted. Compelled by God's grace, Paul wrote more books of the Bible than any other person. Let that sink in. Peter denied Christ three times, but Christ forgave him and commissioned him to help lead the church. Mary Magdalene, a woman who had lived a life of prostitution, received the grace of God into her heart, and she became one of the key followers of Christ. In fact, the first person Christ appeared to on that Easter morning was Mary. Nothing is ever wasted in God's economy. God's grace can take your sufferings, both past and present, and transform them into something of deep value in this life and the life to come.

I know what it means to need an undeserved helping of grace. As a young man I spent time in Amsterdam doing short-term mission work with a group of kids from all over the world, including some from right there in Holland. One day I was with some of my friends in the square near Central Station, where a crowd was gathering to hear a musician. Yolanda was one of my Dutch friends there that day. She was a homely girl with one eye missing, wearing a handmade red and yellow sweater with the words "Jesus loves you" knitted across the front. The musician spotted her in the crowd and stopped playing. Trying to get a laugh, he had her stand up and began mocking her. "Jesus loves *you*? Ha ha ha." It was awful. You could feel her humiliation and rejection, but she stood there in that crowd of people and took it.

I sat frozen in the back row of the crowd, doing nothing to defend my friend. Finally, one brave Dutch guy from our group stood up beside Yolanda and put his arm around her. What a moment. It changed the atmosphere. What a bold move. Me? I just sat there. Pathetic. I went on to do my summer "mission" work that day. The memory of this failure in my past still grieves me. I will never forget that day. The guilt and shame still haunt me over thirty years later. I betrayed my friend, my sister. In doing so, I betrayed Christ.

The only way I survived that moment and that memory is through the lens of grace. I blew it that day in a big way, but God's grace is bigger than my failure. Just like I stumbled and fell that day, you will stumble and fall as you survive these days. That's why we must continue to see our days and lives through the lens of grace or we will be tempted to give up. Don't give up. God's grace picks us up off the floor and gives us that strength to move forward.

THE INSANITY OF TRYING TO EARN THE GRACE OF GOD

One of the wonderful things about grace is that it's not just for beginners. For too long, I thought grace was just for those "sinners" who need to be forgiven and "born again." But the truth of the matter is we all need God's grace every day. This does not mean that we get saved over and over again but that we need to remind ourselves that our acceptance, forgiveness, and standing before God are always based on His grace.

Often on our spiritual trek, we start off enjoying the amazing grace of God on a regular basis. But somewhere along the way, we get tripped up, and instead of relating to God on the level of grace, we revert back to a performance mentality. We live by the lie that says, "We are saved by grace, but we earn God's blessings in our daily lives by our works." In other words, grace is for unbelievers and the law is for believers. Nothing could be further from the truth.

Sometimes I slip back into the performance mentality before I speak at a conference or in church. As I get up to speak, I catch myself checking my spiritual pulse: *Let's see, did I pray today? Did I read my Bible? Did I witness to the person seated next to me on the plane?* On some occasions, I'll think, *This is going to be a lousy message. There is no way God could bless this after all the things I did today, and not to mention the things I didn't do as well.* Other times, I'll reason, *Hmm … it's been a great day. I read my Bible, prayed (on my knees no less), and even took out the trash. God is certainly going to smile on my message today!* In both situations, I relate to God on the basis of my performance instead of His grace. In scenario number one, I feel like I have forfeited God's blessing, and in scenario number two, I feel like I have merited His blessing.

God never intended for us to relate to Him on the basis of our good-day or bad-day performance. Our performance is never good

GOD'S GRACE provides us

with the **ABILITY**

to **ACCEPT OURSELVES,**

WARTS and **ALL,**

to **KNOW** that **HE LOVES US**

and **FORGIVES US**

and **INVITES US**

into **HIS FAMILY**.

enough to be acceptable to Him. Jerry Bridges said it so beautifully in his book *The Discipline of Grace*. He wrote, "Your worst days are never so bad that you are beyond the *reach* of God's grace. And your best days are never so good that you are beyond the *need* of God's grace."[2] Grace is not just for beginners; it is also for you and for me.

God knows that we need His grace from start to finish. We need His grace every single day of our lives. Grace by which we are saved; grace by which we stand. That's why it's called "amazing grace" and not "contingent grace." That's why it's the most powerful force in the universe. God's grace provides us with the ability to accept ourselves, warts and all, to know that He loves us and forgives us and invites us into His family.

When you are struggling to make it through the day, you will make many mistakes along the way. When you find yourself in circumstances beyond your control, you feel helpless and at the mercy of other people. You will get angry, depressed, and fly off the handle at times. You will feel like your circumstances will never improve and you will wonder why this is all happening to you. You are trying to do the right thing and survive in a godly way, but you will fall. When you fail, God's grace and forgiveness are there. He forgives you and accepts you. He's already provided a way out, a means for your forgiveness, which is through the grace of Christ. This grace allows you to own your failings, flaws, and floundering along the way. We need God's grace every single day, because every single day no one follows God perfectly. Embracing our own flaws and imperfections is actually a way we can grow in this survival journey.

PREACH THE GOSPEL TO YOURSELF EVERY DAY

The grace of God carried me through days, weeks, and years of dangers, toils, and snares. The grace of God continues to transform my life. Grace carries me through dark times. Grace covers me despite my imperfections. Grace connects me into this relationship that I was made for—a relationship with the God of the universe. A relationship that's so close I can call Him my Father, my Abba Father.

Grace communicates to me the passionate love of God. From the cradle to the grave, it's all grace. Even beyond, it's the grace of God—His endless favor that forgives, cleanses, and empowers us to live a life for Him, for others. In other words, we were brought into this world to live, breathe, and enjoy God's creation. God provided that environment for us. Our parents or guardians fed us and clothed us and sent us to school. That's grace; we did not deserve any of that. Then we realized that we needed divine grace, and at some point we chose to trust in Christ in a personal way. Later as we grew up and faced challenges, we realized that we require this grace on a daily basis to affirm that we are accepted and loved by God, who provides everything we need. That's why I say it's all grace.

Grace is psychologically healthy. It enables me to live with myself. All of me. My dark side, my hypocritical side, my judgmental side that I fight. It helps me reconcile my Shadow Voice, or the shadow self we all must contend with. The Shadow Voice wants us to dwell on our flaws, sins, and mistakes. This voice condemns us as frauds and phonies, people who are not worthy. The Stronger Voice is the grace of God. Grace will have the final word. The Stronger Voice convinces us that, "Yes, I do have flaws and make mistakes; at the same time God's grace is bigger than my sins. That's the whole point. It's the sick that need a doctor. Jesus came for the sick."

Martin Luther explained it so well when he said we are both saints and sinners: "A Christian is someone who is simultaneously righteous, yet sinful."[3] Think about that. I am accepted because of His righteousness; that's a gift from God. Yet I still have ongoing sin in my life. I don't like it. I hate it. I wish it weren't there, but it is. With grace I fight to overcome it. The apostle Paul first said it, similarly, "But God demonstrates his own love for us in this: *While we were still sinners*, Christ died for us" (Romans 5:8).

As I go through this day, I can live in the embrace of the God who knows me and loves me because of His grace. The circumstances in my life may stink, the pain is still there, the awareness of my own flaws is there, but so is God.

RADICALLY ACCEPT GOD'S RADICAL ACCEPTANCE

In order to survive the day, we have to radically accept our circumstances, no matter how dark or difficult they may be. At the same time, we must radically accept God's radical acceptance. Grace doesn't make sense in our minds or in our world. It's a paradigm from beyond. It transcends and offends our ideas of justice and of earning what we receive in this life. Nothing can erase our past, but grace can cover it. Nothing can take away all of our pain, but grace can comfort us in the midst of it. Nothing can take away the pressure of this world, but grace can empower us to overcome it. One day at a time.

I grew up in the church. I went to Sunday school and "big" church every weekend. I gave money, read my Bible, prayed, told my friends about God. But for many years, I overlooked the grace of God. I heard about God's grace. I sang about God's grace. I said I believed in God's grace. But I actually missed the grace of God. Looking back from where I am now, I can see how life without the grace of God is miserable. Without grace, following God in an attempt to serve Him is sheer drudgery. Life without the grace of God filled me with a self-righteous, judgmental spirit.

It took a long time for me to understand and live from a place of grace. The grace of God was and is the game changer for me. Through grace I felt the love of God and love of others. Through grace I felt the freedom to worship. Through grace I felt more compassion and empathy. By grace I now know I am deeply loved. By grace I know I am accepted. By grace I know I am weak, and yet I am strong. I am empowered by His grace. By grace I can live in gratitude and thanksgiving.

THE WONDER OF GOD'S EMBRACE

When you are in the thick of a survival battle, there are so many decisions you have to make. Loved ones, finances, and the future hang in the balance, and it's easy to revert to a performance-based mentality. In other words, you feel that everything rides on your ability to perform perfectly in order to survive the day and make it through. This kind of thinking will wear you out because it is unrealistic and unsustainable. Besides, that's not how God desires for us to live day to day.

Wherever you are in this moment, whether you are reading or listening to these words, God's grace is available to you. Call out to God right now and say, "God, I desire to know and to receive this grace of Christ in my heart and mind in this moment. Help me to receive this unconditional love right now." Or simply say, "God, I want to experience Your grace and love in a fresh way. I am open to Your love and grace. Fill me in this moment." God will reveal His love to you. He already has at the cross. And you can experience that grace again each and every day.

I needed grace throughout my darkest days. I still need grace. We all need grace. And my understanding and experience of God's love comes to me through this grace. I don't know how to distinguish between God's love and God's grace; they are one and the same to me.

"The most wonderful thing that can happen to any human being is to be loved," wrote spiritual formations teacher Richard Foster. "It alone speaks to the gnawing sense of insignificance and isolation we feel. And the marvelous news is that we have been loved and we are loved, each and every one of us. Uniquely and individually. At the heart of the universe is love, divine love, personal, intimate God-love for you and for me. We are known! We are chosen! Once experienced at the deepest levels of the soul, no reality can be more profoundly disturbing, more radically healing, more utterly transforming."[4]

How wonderful it is to live in God's embrace. To know, no matter how tough, how brutal any day is, we are deeply loved and cherished by the God who made us and knows us. All of this love flows to us through grace, God's action to us and for us. Our past, our pain, the pressure of this moment will not have the final word. Grace will. Love will. When we choose to receive grace, we find ourselves in God's embrace. We know we are forgiven. We are accepted. We are loved by God. He sees us and knows our struggles.

During one of my most brutal seasons, God expressed His love to me, unexpected. I will never forget it. I sat in my bedroom alone with the weight of my world that had shattered. My family was torn apart, my future was in jeopardy, my daughters were not at the house where we raised them. I felt utterly alone. Emptiness, pain, and loneliness flooded my heart. It started to rain outside, pouring rain you could hear hitting the roof, thunder clapping, and the lightning flashing through the windows. At the time, my life was shattered and my future uncertain. And in the midst of that storm, there was an overwhelming sense of God's love for me. In that moment, that broken moment, I knew God was with me and I knew in the depths of my soul that God loved me.

That was a moment of radical grace for me. There was no promise that my life would get better or my circumstances would change, but the promise that God loved me was real and true. That helped me survive that day and many days to come. I can say with confidence His love and grace for you are real in this moment. It

HE SCRIBBLED the words **"I LOVE YOU"** on the **CROSS** by sending **HIS SON** to **SACRIFICE** **HIS LIFE** for **US. JESUS** is **GOD'S UP-CLOSE AND PERSONAL LOVE** to **US.**

may be storming in your life now, but God's love is constant. He loves you because He chose to do so. He loves you in this tough, imperfect moment, and that's grace.

Those last months my mom was in the hospital, she could not talk, could not walk. She could not paint me a picture, so she did what she could. She wrote those simple but deep words "I love you." Through the pain she spoke to my soul. I took a pen, and under her words, I wrote, "I love you too. Very much."

God is love. Through the pain of the cross, and even the pain of our struggle to make it, God speaks to our soul too. He scribbled the words "I love you" on the cross by sending His Son to sacrifice His life for us. Jesus is God's up-close and personal love to us.

SURVIVAL PRAYER:

Father, I receive Your acceptance and embrace today. Thank You for Your grace that shows me I am deeply loved by You in this moment. My goal today is not to be perfect, but to be faithful and a joyful recipient of Your amazing grace.

SURVIVAL PASSAGE:

This is how God showed his love among us: He sent his one and only Son into the world that we might live through him. This is love: not that we loved God, but that he loved us and sent his Son as an atoning sacrifice for our sins.

1 John 4:9–10

SURVIVAL PRACTICE:

Open your hands this morning, at lunch, and before you go to sleep tonight, and say out loud, "I receive Your grace in this moment, Lord."

CHAPTER EIGHT

ESTAMOS CONTENTOS

"Radical acceptance rests on letting go of the illusion of control and a willingness to notice and accept things as they are right now, without judging."

Marsha Linehan

Years ago, I lived in Mexico City for an entire summer working with an indigenous church-planting movement, supporting local Mexican pastors to start churches throughout the country. I went out and spent each day with local pastors and met the people we wanted to help. We went *puerta a puerta*, "door to door," talking to people about the gospel, inviting them to church, praying for them.

One particular Wednesday is etched in my memory. I spent the day with Pastor Josef. He was thirty-five years old, tall, black hair, and a mustache. He once lived in the United States but moved back to Mexico after his conversion experience. We had several meaningful conversations about his coming to Christ while in the States and his desire to go back to Mexico to be a pastor. He was a sincere guy who believed deeply in the grace of God. We had walked door to door that day, witnessing in the poor neighborhood where he was planting the church.

At around 5:00 p.m., we walked down a dirt road and came upon a tin structure that looked like the kind of shed you would use to store a lawn mower and yard tools back in the States. It wasn't a storage shed, though. It was Josef's house. One room with dirt floors, a sheet dividing the main area from the place where the family slept. His wife greeted us at the door with an infant in her arms. Then we sat down at the kitchen table, where I noticed a new Thompson Chain-Reference Bible lying in front of us. I was shocked that they lived in this place, and I guess Josef sensed my bewilderment. He turned and looked me in the eye and said, *"Estamos contentos, hermano. Estamos contentos"*—which means "We are content, my brother. We are content." Finding contentment in such conditions is not easy. I was humbled by his simple but clear declaration of their happy state in their simple home.

Peace and contentment in the midst of poverty and lack? He sincerely meant what he said. He was thankful for his family, the roof over his head, and the Bible on the table. Somewhere along the way, my friend Josef had found the secret to contentment.

The path to peace and contentment in the midst of a storm is found in surrender. Surrender is about letting go of the people, the problems, and the circumstances in our lives that we have

THE PATH to PEACE and

CONTENTMENT in the

MIDST of a STORM is

FOUND in SURRENDER.

no control over. Surrender means letting go, trusting God, and moving forward in life regardless of the outcome or consequences. However, the way of surrender is hard to come by and rarely found. We may humble ourselves, receive God's grace, and yet avoid surrendering as long as possible because we hang on to control with every fiber, muscle, and bone in our bodies.

THE HIGH COST OF CONTROL

Most of us possess a natural desire to control our circumstances and the people in our lives, especially when times are tough. Living in an ever-changing world, fraught with complexity and uncertainty, it's normal to want to hold on to control in our little corner of it. Whether we desire to control our career, our family, our spouse, our kids, our body, or the outcome of a particular project, we sometimes live in the illusion that we really are in control. Of course, some aspects of control are necessary, but far too often we fall prey to an inordinate obsession to control others and our circumstances.

A *Psychology Today* article states, "In our search to gain more control over ourselves and our lives we frequently and foolishly seek to control other people. But to attempt to control others, while perhaps making life more convenient, is also to attempt to curtail their autonomy."[1] Chris Sandel is a nutritional therapist who works with people who have difficult relationships with food and their bodies. Because we are inextricably connected to our bodies and what we put into them, he has some keen insights on the subject of control and influence. He argues that we must differentiate between influence and control, and that can be such a fine line. He says, "I tend to think of 'control' as where someone has an outcome in mind and they believe that they have total ability to create this exact outcome. Influence on the other hand is where someone has an outcome in mind and they know that there are things that make it more likely for this to happen but in reality there are factors outside of their control that mean there are no guarantees."[2]

When we hold on to the illusion of control, we miss out on honestly connecting with others, shared pain, shared joy, meaningful work, and time with family, friends, and of course, God. Perhaps this problem has become the soundtrack of your life. It's like we are wearing headphones that keep pumping our minds full of doom and gloom. The voice in the headphones fills our hearts with anxiety and fear, which makes us feel out of control, which then leads us to try to control the things and people around us.

We need to stop and take time to evaluate our beliefs and behaviors. Most of our motivations are so far beneath the surface we don't even realize they are driving us. We may sincerely believe that we are demonstrating how much we love a certain person by sacrificing everything for them—our time, our money, our emotional space. We become convinced that we are laying down our life for this person. Loving like Jesus. Picking up our cross. Helping them. We may be consumed with helping them. We may have an *I-can-fix-it* mentality. Or we may honestly believe we "can't let them ruin their own life."

Another unhealthy way we may cope is by holding on and grieving the memory of someone we have lost for an inordinate length of time. We believe we are honoring them by not moving on with our own life. How can we be happy when others are so sad and hurting? We find meaning in being sad and depressed. Unfortunately, there's a payoff for lingering in sadness and depression without seeking help. There's a payoff in control and martyrdom. We get to play the "poor me" card. The bottom line of that payoff is that we don't have to be responsible for our experience of life.

But we have to stop and realize what it's costing us to hold on to our version of control. The cost may be money, happiness, joy, and friendship. So often we want to control things we cannot control. Control is an illusion with a high price tag. There are many things we cannot control or we're not supposed to control. We know that, but we still hang on with all of our might. Many times we are holding on for the sake of a marriage, a son, a daughter, or a close friend. We tend to think control will bring us peace and freedom from pain, but believe me, there's a better path to take.

THE FREEDOM OF SURRENDER

Reinhold Niebuhr wrote one of the most powerful, life-giving prayers ever penned, known commonly as the "Serenity Prayer." Reinhold and his brother Richard were influential theologians who impacted Christians all over the world during the twentieth century. Many recovery groups now recite the first part of this prayer to close their meetings. You may know it by heart, "God, give me grace to accept with serenity the things that cannot be changed, courage to change the things which should be changed, and the wisdom to distinguish the one from the other." It's a reminder to accept life on its own terms and to peacefully find realistic solutions to your problems. But as wonderful as the first part of this prayer is, the best part is in the second half, which most people never see or hear. "Living one day at a time; enjoying one moment at a time; accepting hardship as a pathway to peace; taking, as Jesus did, this sinful world as it is, not as I would have it; trusting that You will make all things right, if I surrender to Your will; so that I may be reasonably happy in this life, and supremely happy with You forever in the next."

There it is. The invitation to live in the moment, let the day unfold, don't get ahead of yourself, live one day at a time. To paraphrase Niebuhr, he says to embrace hardships and radically accept this broken, fallen world as it is; don't buy the lie that you can create heaven on earth. It ain't gonna happen! Then he closes with the secret: surrender to God's will for your life. Surrender and you will find "reasonable happiness." I love Niebuhr's realism and how he gives hope by pointing to supreme happiness in the next life with God. If we can live the words of that prayer, just one day at a time, our lives and our perception of this world will radically change. Surrender will enable us to survive the day in a powerful way—a way that places us in the center of God's will, to live for Him and to serve others with the gifts and talents He has given us.

As freeing as surrender is, it always comes with a price that never goes on sale. We are often brought into the way of surrender by being thrown into painful circumstances that feel like they will never end. This pain and helplessness thrust us into the arms of God and into the place of surrender.

UNFAILING STRENGTH

Two of the most dynamic leaders I've ever known are Edd and Nina Hendee. They run a large, successful restaurant in Houston. They are hardworking, God-fearing people, the epitome of what it means to be servant leaders. They selflessly, with no fanfare, help hurting people behind the scenes all over the world. Several years ago, they lost their only son to a skiing accident. He was only thirty-three years old, a former naval officer with a young wife and three precious children.

After their son died, Edd and Nina invited their daughter-in-law and their grandchildren to live with them in their house in Houston. They arranged the entire second floor to be a home for their son's young family. Edd is one of the strongest men you will ever meet, physically, mentally, and spiritually. As the entire family was undergoing intense grief under the same roof, Edd didn't know how he was going to make it through the day. He shared, "The mountain I had to climb was too high and too steep, I just couldn't do it."

Despite his grief, he made a commitment to get up every morning and start his day with a cup of coffee, Bible reading, and prayer. And every day Edd surrendered it all to God. He turned it over to the only One who could give him the strength and power to make it through this painful, dark season.

After six months, he felt the need to get a medical checkup, to monitor his health during this difficult time. He told his doctor these were the hardest months of his life. The doctor took Edd's blood pressure. In disbelief, he took it again. And much to their surprise, his blood pressure was lower than it had been at his last visit. Somehow, God sustained Edd's health as he surrendered it all to Him.

We do not know what tomorrow holds, but we do know that God holds tomorrow. That He will be in our tomorrows and give us the strength, power, and even contentment one day at a time. All of it flows to us through this way of surrender. *Estamos contentos.*

CONTROL IS AN ILLUSION

One of my dearest friends in the world runs a massive missions organization that plants churches in some of the most dangerous places in the world. His organization reaches into what the Great Commission calls the uttermost parts of the world. But several years ago, my friend collapsed while watching a high school basketball game. People gathered around him, prayed for him, and rushed him to the hospital. Everyone thought he must have had a heart attack. He survived the day and then went through a battery of tests to try to find out what had happened. The doctors ruled out heart attack, stroke, brain cancer, all of the things that could cause such a sudden collapse. Finally, they concluded he'd had a panic attack.

Afterward, he consulted the best doctors and psychologists he could find, he traveled across the country in search of a cause, read books about it, tried to change his diet. He did everything you would do if you experienced such a sudden collapse.

Later as more panic attacks occurred, he went down his own checklist, asking himself, is there anything in my life that's not right? Is there a moral problem? A physical problem? An emotional problem? The panic attacks did not go away. For months he tried everything under the sun to come out of this state and feel better. He tried all the common-sense stuff and then all the weird stuff, but none of it helped. Finally, he felt like God was saying to him, "Instead of trying to feel better, why don't you start trusting Me more?"

So he did. He surrendered. He let go and submitted it completely to God. He came to the conclusion that control was an illusion and surrender was the only way to attain peace. My friend is one of the most godly guys I know and, at the same time, one of the most driven. He's a spiritual giant to me and countless others, but even he had to go through the ongoing pain of panic attacks to get to a point of total surrender. And now you might assume he's living a victorious life and everything is better … Nope. That's not what happened. It actually got worse.

He was suddenly stricken with Bell's palsy, a condition that paralyzes half of your face, which is pretty debilitating for someone who talks for a living. When the palsy didn't go away like the experts predicted, he thought, *I am not going to waste the majority of this trial trying to feel better, but I am going to surrender up front and trust God with it.*

Don't misunderstand the point here. He still did everything the doctor ordered, but his mind-set and emotions were different. He surrendered. *Estamos contentos.*

THE SECRET OF SURRENDER

By far, the most painful aspect of divorce is the impact it has on the kids. It can be relentless. By God's grace my two daughters are in a good place now. They are as beautiful on the inside as they are on the outside. They are smart and talented, and I am immensely proud of them. But for years when they were younger, understandably, they struggled to cope with the new, brutal reality of living in a divided home.

My stress level and anxiety reached such a peak three years after the divorce that my health started to deteriorate. I was sick and couldn't seem to get well. My kids were struggling to deal with life, being bounced back and forth between their mom and dad. I still went to see my therapists every single week. I was desperately trying to control my life and my kids' lives, but my body was physically shutting down. I had trouble sleeping. I had trouble eating. I cried out to God as I lay flat on my face on the floor of my house. The emotional pain was too great. Fear flooded my heart, and I reached the end of myself. I did not want to carry on. In a moment of anger, I grabbed my Bible that I read every day and hurled it across the room. Then I fell flat on my face and cried my eyes out. I don't know how I was able to cry, or how I had any more tears left, because I had already cried for about three years straight prior to that day.

At my next therapist appointment, he gave me an analogy that made a lot of sense. He said it was like one of my kids was drowning, and as I went to save one, the other kid started to drown as well. Then when I went to save the other kid, I noticed that they were attached underwater by a rope, and as a matter of fact, we were all attached by the same rope and all of us were drowning. That stuck with me.

And on a Thursday night, when I felt like I could carry on no more, I quit. I completely quit. I quit trying to control my life, my kids' lives, my health. I surrendered. I had to. I was dying. In that moment, somehow I knew if there was any way I could ever hope to influence and help my kids in the future, I had to be alive to do it. So I surrendered it all to God.

Let me answer your next question. No, my life and circumstances did not get better in that moment. They actually got worse on many levels, but I now had a new sense of contentment, a strange peace that God was with me and He was with my kids. I turned them over to God as I turned myself over to God. My love and provision for them did not change a bit. I did not give up my responsibility as their dad at all. In fact, I hope I became a better dad at that moment. I just let go. I stopped trying to play God.

As a parent, your instinct is to do everything possible to help your children. There's nothing I wouldn't have done for my daughters. I discovered much wisdom from therapists and books that helped me shift how I saw my role as a parent during that time.

I read so many books. Melody Beattie's books in particular were instrumental in my path of surrender. She wrote in one of them, "Letting go doesn't mean we don't care. Letting go doesn't mean we shut down. Letting go means we stop trying to force outcomes."[3] That bit of wisdom helped to relieve me of some of the incorrect thinking that had kept me paralyzed.

Though previously I had believed my motives and heart were in the right place, I was trying too hard to control and manipulate the outcome. I had to allow my daughters to make their own choices and to live their own lives, even though they were so young. That's how I learned the brutal and heart-wrenching secret of surrender. I was dragged into it kicking and screaming. Crying out to God and to my friends, I simply gave up and gave it all to Him. Letting go is never easy, and not always painless, but it is freeing. And it's essential in our relationship with God. Surrender is an inestimable key to surviving the day. Even kicking and screaming, *estamos contentos*.

FLYING TRAPEZE AND SURRENDER

When I was a little boy, my family vacationed for a week in a place called Callaway Gardens in Georgia. There at the resort was the Florida State University Circus—the only circus program in the world located at a university. Learn to juggle and get your bachelor of arts degree all under the big top.

One of the groups performing was the trapeze artists. Amazing, flying through the air with the greatest of ease. Trapezetry is a team effort. It takes a minimum of two people to make it happen.

But surprisingly, the most important person is not the one who's doing somersaults and flips in midair without a net. Of course, they're important. But who we usually take for granted is the all-important catcher. The flyer has to let go. Then the flyer must trust the catcher. Even when the catcher comes into plain view, the flyer can do nothing except allow the catcher to catch her. The flyer lets go. The flyer trusts. The catcher does the rest. Timing. Waiting. But the flyer must first let go.[4]

You may not feel like a flyer or a trapeze artist. Maybe the only thing you can relate to is that your life feels like a circus that's way out of control. But you have to let go and trust the catcher. That's what my friends did. That's what I've done. Let go and trust the catcher will hold on to you.

The day I threw my Bible across the room in a fit of rage, pain, and grief, after I stopped sobbing on the carpet, I got up, walked over, and picked my Bible up off of the floor. Some pages were bent and folded back, dog eared, pit-bull style. The passage it was opened to was this: "Praise be to the God and Father of our Lord Jesus Christ, the Father of compassion and the God of all comfort, who comforts us in all our troubles, so that we can comfort those in any trouble with the comfort we ourselves receive from God" (2 Corinthians 1:3–4).

In that devastating moment, God was there; He was with me. God comforted me and brought me through. In an instant, I felt comforted like a child wrapped up in his daddy's arms. Perhaps this is my gift to you—the comfort He gave me I want to pass on to you. I don't want to waste my sorrows or allow my pain to be in vain. As others brought comfort to me, I hope this word of hope and grace brings comfort to you.

Now that you understand the choices available to you, it's time to implement them so that you, too, can find peace in the midst of life's storms.

SURVIVAL PRAYER:

The Serenity Prayer by Reinhold Niebuhr

God, give me grace to accept with serenity
the things that cannot be changed,
Courage to change the things
which should be changed,
and the wisdom to distinguish
the one from the other.

Living one day at a time,
Enjoying one moment at a time,
Accepting hardship as a pathway to peace,
Taking, as Jesus did,
This sinful world as it is,
Not as I would have it,
Trusting that You will make all things right,
If I surrender to Your will,
So that I may be reasonably happy in this life,
And supremely happy with You forever in the next.
Amen.

SURVIVAL PASSAGE:

"Father, if you are willing, take this cup from me; yet not my will, but yours be done." An angel from heaven appeared to him and strengthened him. And being in anguish, he prayed more earnestly, and his sweat was like drops of blood falling to the ground.

Luke 22:42–44

SURVIVAL PRACTICE:

Call a friend today and tell him or her how you have surrendered your situation to God. Tell your friend what that means to you and why you had to do it.

PART THREE

THE CHANGE TO
MOVE FORWARD

CHAPTER NINE

WIN THE MORNING

"It comes the very moment you wake up each morning.
All your wishes and hopes for the day rush at you like
wild animals. And the first job each morning consists
simply in shoving them all back; in listening to that
other voice, taking that other point of view, letting that
other larger, stronger, quieter life come flowing in."

C. S. Lewis

My family is crazy about basketball. My two brothers and I
played in high school, and my oldest brother played college ball
at Florida State. We spent our formative years shooting hoops
in damp gymnasiums or in our backyard. Growing up in the
basketball country of North and South Carolina, we competed
against some of the toughest teams in the nation. One of my
most cherished memories of the game involves the creative cheers
from our opponents' fans and cheerleaders. Whenever you shot
a free throw, the cheerleaders would chant, "U-G-L-Y, you ain't

got no alibi. You're ugly. Boy, you're ugly." Or if they really hated you, they would add, "Your mama says, 'You're ugly.'" *My mama said that?*

Another cheer still rings in my mind today. It's not a derogatory or ad hominem attack but a word of encouragement, almost a compliment, when you got the ball on offense. It goes like this: "You got it. Now use it. You got it. Now use it." I love this cheer, which is simple, yet powerful. Mark Twain once wrote, "I can live two weeks on a good compliment."[1] Sometimes just a positive word of grace or truth is enough to empower us to make it through the day. We all need encouragement.

Now it's my turn to cheer you on. You've got it! You've got how to survive the day in a powerful way, and now that you've got it, you must use it. Let's apply what we know, survive the day, and watch God work in us and through us.

Earlier I mentioned my passion for the practice of Brazilian jiu-jitsu. BJJ has taught me many life lessons. In the early years as a white belt, I didn't yet have the skills to dominate and win, but I did learn how to survive. How to breathe. How to remain as calm as possible under stressful and life-threatening situations. They were simulated perils but good practice for the real thing. This applies to our daily survival as well. In a life crisis, we can't just hit the eject button and launch ourselves out of danger or discomfort. Sometimes we remain under duress for extended periods of time. So we have to adapt. We learn to breathe deeply and lower our heart rate.

How can we get a little more comfortable in an uncomfortable situation? How can we breathe, move, remain as calm as

Sometimes just a

POSITIVE WORD OF

GRACE OR TRUTH

is **ENOUGH TO**

EMPOWER US to make

it through the day.

possible, and survive the day? We have to find ways of coping that suit us in order to learn endurance during hardship.

This is also the case in ordinary life. But especially when we are in a long-term survival or recovery mode, it is important that we put ourselves in a position to succeed. When I first started going to therapy, I was surprised and a bit annoyed at the three questions one therapist always started with. "Are you sleeping? Are you eating? Are you working out?"

Are you sleeping?

Are you eating?

Are you working out?

Honestly, I thought, *Seriously, this is what I pay you for? I've got bigger problems than this!* But of course, she was right. She knew before I did that I was not in a short-term predicament, and I came to appreciate the long-term strategy of being on top of the basics (which was really all I could control anyway!). Our natural tendency in duress is to neglect the basic things that keep us alive and thinking clearly. I became very committed to these three basic things (consistent sleep pattern, good nutrition, and exercise), and I was amazed at the amount of good it did for me.

Jiu-jitsu is a lot like chess, in that you're constantly plotting how you can turn your opponent's offensive moves to your advantage. Some might say you want to use negative energy in a positive way. It's a strategy that can help you survive in life too. We see this manifested in Joseph's life when, after his years of suffering at his brothers' hands, he responded with "You meant evil against me, but God meant it for good" (Genesis 50:20 ESV).

Even in the midst of a storm of suffering, God is working for our good.

Even though we may not see Him or understand our circumstances, God is at work. No one wants to miss what almighty God is doing because we are so distracted by the details around us. "God, don't let me miss what You are trying to do" is a frequent prayer of mine. Sometimes I get caught up in my circumstances and I have to catch myself. "God, open my eyes to what You are doing here." I have to surrender my ways to His ways. "'For my thoughts are not your thoughts, neither are your ways my ways,' declares the LORD. 'As the heavens are higher than the earth, so are my ways higher than your ways and my thoughts than your thoughts'" (Isaiah 55:8–9). Sometimes God's greatest work comes out of suffering.

So what about you, my friend? Are you sleeping? Are you eating? Are you working out? Take good care of your physical well-being and notice how much your outlook on life improves.

OTHER PRACTICAL TOOLS

Sometimes just a simple word of grace or truth is enough to empower us to make it through the day. We all need encouragement. And sometimes that encouragement springs from unusual places and memories. You might hear a song that speaks to your heart or receive an uplifting message from a friend. The message in a Sunday sermon may spark hope or even make you laugh. Be expectant that God will bring just what you need to see or hear day by day.

As I have struggled, cried, and battled to make it through difficult days that kept growing more complicated and seasons that seemed to grow darker instead of brighter, I've tried to keep some simple reminders. A few passages of Scripture helped me through the hard days. Psalm 86 and 1 Peter 5 were always close by. "Cast all your anxiety on him because he cares for you" (1 Peter 5:7). Words of wisdom from various people helped me to keep moving forward in my life and not live in the pain of the past. One of my favorite quotes that kept my perspective healthy and my momentum going forward is by Søren Kierkegaard. I've mentioned it before, but it bears repeating. He wisely said, "Life can only be understood backwards, but it must be lived forwards." I'd leave note cards around with quotes that reminded me that painful circumstances and suffering were not without meaning and could actually be making me stronger.

At times when I felt alone and that no one could possibly understand what I was going through, I would read Hebrews 12:1–3: "Therefore, since we are surrounded by such a great cloud of witnesses …" Someone once taught me when you see a *therefore* in the Bible, always ask, "What's it *there for*?" Usually it refers back to what preceded the passage. In this case, the "cloud of witnesses" is referring back to what many scholars call the "Hall of Fame of Faith." It includes men and women such as Abraham, Sarah, Moses, and Rahab who endured excruciatingly painful days, months, and years by holding on to their trust in God against all odds. I like to picture them in the grandstands cheering for us. "You got it. Now use it!" "I made it through, so you can make it through!" "Keep moving forward, trusting God." They are cheering us on.

All of these hall of famers were surrendered to God. Remember this. We are surrounded by the surrendered. They surround us every morning when our feet hit the floor. Every day as we take on our battles, they are cheering us on. Every time we feel overwhelmed or depressed, they surround us. Move forward with God. Stay humble. Receive His amazing grace, and surrender—turn it all over to God. They are shouting words of encouragement.

I've added other people to my Hall of Fame of Faith. I imagine C. S. Lewis is in the stands for me. My godly grandfather who was in a wheelchair most of my life is now standing in the stands for me. My mom, who recently died, is definitely in the stands for me. Even Kierkegaard is in the stands for me, along with a host of others. Find people in the Bible, in history, and in your daily life whom you admire or love, and picture them in the stands for you, yelling, cheering, loving, and believing in you to the finish line.

The following Hebrews passage is so rich with practical help for our survival that it's worth mining its meaning by breaking it down.

"Let us throw off everything that hinders and the sin that so easily entangles" (Hebrews 12:1a). Throw off the worries, anxieties, and burdens that weigh you down and keep you from trusting God. Get rid of everything unnecessary to survive the day. The goal is to be lean and agile spiritually. Confess and deal with any ongoing sin in your life. Dig up any pride, greed, jealousy, envy, and temptation, and deal with it. Stop trying to save and rescue people who really don't want to be helped. We all have things weighing us down that we need to throw off.

"And let us run with perseverance the race marked out for us" (Hebrews 12:1b). We run this race and we survive this day with a mind-set of endurance. We need a marathon mentality to make it through this day and then the next. We all have our own hurdles we must clear to make it through this day. It's not a quick sprint; it's our God-given race. It's our challenge and our life that we must rise up to with humility, grace, and surrender in order to run the best race we can. One step at a time. One day at a time.

"Fixing our eyes on Jesus, the pioneer and perfecter of faith" (Hebrews 12:2a). Jesus is the one who started our journey with God, and He is the one who will empower us to the finish line. "He who began a good work in you will carry it on to completion" (Philippians 1:6). Jesus is the one who knows our troubles, the one who came for us, the one who lived for us, and the one who died for us. When we fix our eyes on Him rather than on all the problems and stressors, we gain a more positive perspective on life.

"For the joy set before him he endured the cross, scorning its shame, and sat down at the right hand of the throne of God" (Hebrews 12:2b). Jesus gives us deep joy in the midst of pain and trials and in the grind of everyday life. He is our example of endurance and perseverance all the way to the cross. He humbled Himself before God the Father and laid down His life for us. He surrendered, "Not my will, but yours be done" (Luke 22:42).

All for us, that we might be forgiven, restored, and invited into the family of God. And now He's at the right hand of the Father. He is sitting, which means His work is finished. He is the way to the Father; He is the grace we need. We can approach God's throne with grace and bring our sins and our thorns to Him.

"Consider him who endured such opposition from sinners, so that you will not grow weary and lose heart" (Hebrews 12:3). There were so many times in my life when I wanted to quit. Times when I lost heart and wanted to give up. There were times when I questioned why I was suffering, even though I knew Jesus had suffered. Jesus set the example of how to suffer well, with grace and humility and an attitude of surrender. I pray that God would not waste our sorrows and suffering but that He would work in and through them. When we remember the cross with gratitude, we gain strength so as not to lose heart in our battles.

WIN THE MORNING

Bestselling author and success coach Tim Ferriss said, "If you win the morning, you win the day."[2] That's good advice! If we want to survive the day in a powerful way, it starts the minute we wake up. First thing in the morning, set your mind and heart in a winning way. Even if it's just for a few minutes. I like to grab a cup of coffee and find a quiet place.

In the early days of working through my crisis, I made it a habit to get up when it was still dark outside. The gradual transition from dark to dawn to daylight became symbolic of the hope of a new day. It reminds me of the reality that darkness is not a permanent state of being. That things change. That hope rises. Experiencing the sunrise each morning lifted my soul and

WHEN WE REMEMBER

the **CROSS** with gratitude,

we **GAIN STRENGTH**

so as

NOT TO LOSE HEART

in our **BATTLES**.

became an important part of my healing. A little bit each day. And each morning as the sun came up, I would start with the truth of God's Word.

I would take a passage of Scripture and pray my way through it. "Clothe yourselves, all of you, with humility toward one another, for 'God opposes the proud but gives grace to the humble.' Humble yourselves, therefore, under the mighty hand of God so that at the proper time he may exalt you" (1 Peter 5:5–6 ESV).

My daily prayers now include humility, grace, and surrender, like this:

HUMILITY. I simply pray, "God, I humble myself before You today. You are God and I am not. You are wiser, more powerful, and You alone are the Source of all knowledge and truth. I am a created being below You, and I depend upon You for my next breath. I am open to learn from You and others today. I see this day as an opportunity to serve others with the gifts and talents You've given me. I am not better than anyone I will see or be with today. We are all equal in Your sight. We are all dependent on You for life. I am under your authority and protection."

GRACE. Next, I ask for God's grace. "Father, thank You for forgiving me. I confess my pride, my greed, my envy, my anger, my judgmental thoughts, and my victim mentality to You. I am a sinner by nature and choice. I need Your forgiveness. Thank You for dying in my place and rising again that I may be accepted in Your sight. Thank You that I am forgiven, accepted, and adopted into Your family and that nothing and no one can snatch me from Your hands and Your care. Thank You for loving me deeply and completely through Your Son. I receive this amazing, transforming, accepting grace. Because You accept me just as I am, I in turn can accept others.

"God, I also receive Your empowering grace today. Thank You for the grace that keeps me centered and focused on You during the tasks that need to be accomplished today. Thank You that Your grace is sufficient for me today, that You will provide the strength and the power that I do not naturally possess. Thank You that Your power, the same power that raised Jesus Christ from the dead, lives in me. Thank You that even though I feel weak and feeble this morning, I know You are strong, which makes me strong in You. God, I set my mind and heart to continually turn to You throughout the day for strength and power. In all the meetings I have, all the appointments, all the interactions with others, I will call upon Your name and Your power to see me through."

SURRENDER. Then I turn it all over to God. "Casting all your anxiety on him because he cares for you" (1 Peter 5:7). I pray, "Lord, I give You my worry and anxiety. I let go of trying to control all the people in my life. I let go of the outcomes and results that I am not responsible for. I surrender. I stop playing god this morning and surrender to do Your will. God, I give You my will in exchange for Your will. I set my heart and mind to do Your will Your way. I choose to work hard for You. I choose to serve others in everything I do. I choose to get my eyes off of myself, my worries, my burdens, and my chaos, and I turn that over to You in order to focus on others. Father, I trust You with everything. You did not make me to understand everything in this life. I give to you all the *whys* so that I may do the *whats* of this very day. Thank You that You do care for me and that You are using all things to make me stronger, wiser, and more equipped to take on the life You have for me today. Thank You for Jesus Christ, who is the incarnation of humility, grace, and surrender. I give everything to You and surrender to You in this moment."

On some mornings I use my hands to symbolize my position before God during these three prayers. I put my hands together and bow my head to show humility before God. I then open my hands palms facing up when I pray through grace, showing that I receive His acceptance and power in this moment. Then I put my hands palms down for surrender, which demonstrates I am giving all of my worries and cares to Him. In doing this, I am laying all of my problems on the altar to surrender to God and to His will.

PUTTING IT ALL TOGETHER

When you think about it, this way of humility, grace, and surrender is not only a good way to survive the day in a powerful way; it's also the way to live your entire life before God. We will never outgrow the need for humility. I will never reach a point in my life in which I no longer need to humble myself before God and others. That day will never come. There will never come a day when I no longer need God's grace. Grace has brought me safely thus far and grace will lead me home. I will be celebrating His grace ten thousand years from now. Maybe I should write a song with these words. Surrender is not a one-time, one-day event, but it's powerful every day. We will never outgrow the need we have to turn our issues over to God.

Life is a continuous journey of surrender and trusting God with the complexities, uncertainties, and trials of this life.

Humility. Grace. Surrender. The practice of these three contexts will get us through the day and this brief thing we call life on this planet. Humility. Grace. Surrender. These are the essence of following Christ and being conformed to His likeness. Think about it. Christ is the incarnation of humility. As He humbled Himself to full obedience, even taking it to the cross, He became the grace of God to us. The grace that covers us, accepts us, forgives us, and empowers us, flows to us and through us by the power of the cross and resurrection. He is the model of surrender.

He surrendered all to the Father, choosing not His will, but His Father's will, so that we might also be connected to the Father. We surrender and we trust because He showed us how to do it. While these are the tools we need to use to survive, they are also the way to live fully. As we practice these essentials of the Christian faith, we are in fact learning to thrive in life again.

Author and professor Jerry Sittser continues to serve as one of the strong voices in my life to help me survive the day with wisdom and strength. He understands the depth of pain, loss, and redemption in a profound way. He wrote about the mysterious nature of this ongoing surrender, this ever-evolving relationship we have with God, saying, "Such is the paradox of the redemptive story—we lose to gain, die to live, renounce to inherit, surrender ourselves to get ourselves back. We gain true freedom only when we surrender it and choose to know, trust, and obey God."[3]

Years ago, in the midst of my near drowning, aka my *What about Bob?* existence, I wrote the following poem. I guess that's what you would call it at least. It helped me stay focused and grounded on what I needed to do each day.

Today

I can't control tomorrow just today.
All I have is today.
Yesterday is gone and tomorrow is not here yet.
I just have today.
Today is a beautiful thing.
Today is a wonderful gift.
All I have is today.
Today I can do the next right thing.
Today I can speak the truth.
Today I can love.
Today I can give.
Today I can help.
Yesterday is gone and tomorrow is not here yet.
I just have today.

When your circumstances seem to engulf you, reread this poem as a prayer and choose humility, grace, and surrender. These three powerful, counterintuitive choices will help you survive the day with God and grow stronger.

SURVIVAL PRAYER:

Father, I thank You for today, not tomorrow, just today. Help me to live one day at a time. Help me to love others, to serve others, and to work at the tasks I have to do. I humble myself before You. I receive Your grace for this day and let go of all of the things in my life I can't control.

SURVIVAL PASSAGE:

> Therefore, since we are surrounded by such a great cloud of witnesses, let us throw off everything that hinders and the sin that so easily entangles. And let us run with perseverance the race marked out for us, fixing our eyes on Jesus, the pioneer and perfecter of faith. For the joy set before him he endured the cross, scorning its shame, and sat down at the right hand of the throne of God. Consider him who endured such opposition from sinners, so that you will not grow weary and lose heart.

Hebrews 12:1–3

SURVIVAL PRACTICE:

Create your own morning ritual that helps you access the three choices of humility, grace, and surrender.

CHAPTER TEN

SILENCING YOUR SHADOW VOICE

"Sow a thought and you reap an action; sow an act and you reap a habit; sow a habit and you reap a character; sow a character and you reap a destiny."

Ralph Waldo Emerson

One of the things I am least proud of in my life is the mess associated with my freshman dorm room at college. The level of filth, clutter, and grime was unimaginable. Old Domino's pizza boxes, McDonald's wrappers, and wadded-up papers covered the floor. We never changed our sheets, so they were permanently cola stained and sprinkled with dirt from our shoes. On "Parents Weekend," I walked down the hall to take a shower. When I returned ten minutes later, a group of moms and dads had swarmed around the door of our room. They were laughing and motioning to other parents to come take a look at how disgustingly messy our domicile had become.

Ironically, the guys who made that mess as freshmen went on to become a pastor, a lawyer, and a United States congressman, who was chairman of the House Oversight Committee. The problem lay in the fact that we normalized all the clutter, chaos, and garbage that littered our room. We tolerated it and lived in it for an entire school year.

When you are striving to make it through a season of difficult days, weeks, or months, your mind can become just as chaotic and unkept as my old dorm room. When you fail to deal with self-condemning thoughts that come from the Shadow Voice, your mind becomes a very unsanitary place. It's easy to fall into a spiritual rut or malaise because you don't get a grip on your destructive, self-condemning thoughts. Instead of dealing with them, we live with the mess and chaos in our heads.

When I attempted to make it through and survive my life storm years ago, the Shadow Voice spoke condemning words to me: *"You're a loser." "Your life is over." "No one will accept you again." "Your kids will be messed up for life." "There's no hope."* I felt afraid of what would happen next. How would I make it emotionally? Financially? Vocationally? I felt hopeless and despondent. Despair was ever present. I wanted to give up. The atmosphere in my mind was dark. Depressing. Anxious. Angry. Brutal. These haunting, destructive words sought to dominate the dialogue in my mind.

All of us have a running conversation going on in our minds on autopilot. We may not even be aware of the destructive words and phrases that we silently repeat to ourselves throughout the day. A random thought may creep into your mind and you'll say to yourself, *I don't have what it takes. I don't know if I'm going to make it. I feel like such a failure. I am inadequate.* When we repeat these thoughts to ourselves continually, we start to believe them, and they affect who we are and how we feel. As we go through our days, we allow these misbeliefs, half-truths, and outright lies to beat us up and pound us down. They bully us.

Dr. Caroline Leaf, a cognitive neuroscientist who specializes in brain neuroplasticity, observes, "What you are thinking every moment of every day becomes a physical reality in your brain and body, which affects your optimal mental and physical health. These thoughts collectively form your attitude, which is your state of mind, and it's *your attitude and not your DNA* that determines much of the quality of your life."[1]

What we tell ourselves daily, or even hourly, affects us physically, emotionally, and psychologically. If we don't stand up to the Shadow Voice, and we allow these condemning lies to embed themselves in our minds, they can have catastrophic effects on our character, our future, and the attitude we take in order to survive the day.

One of the most revolutionary discoveries in the field of psychology is the basic idea that our thoughts and attitudes create our moods. In other words, external events cannot "make" us feel anything; rather, it is our beliefs about these circumstances that affect how we will feel. Of course, God already knew this and wrote about this principle centuries ago, stating, "As [a man] thinketh in

WHAT WE TELL

OURSELVES daily, or

even hourly, AFFECTS

us PHYSICALLY,

EMOTIONALLY, and

PSYCHOLOGICALLY.

his heart, so is he" (Proverbs 23:7 KJV). God wants us to experience freedom. And a lot of freedom that you can experience will happen when you get a grip on what's going on inside your mind and when you stand up to the Bully Brain.

It's imperative you allow the truth of who God is and what He says about you to sink deep inside your heart and mind. The apostle Paul wrote a powerful passage on the Shadow Voice and what to do about it in one of his letters to a group of young, imperfect people in Greece. He wrote, "The weapons we fight with are not the weapons of the world. On the contrary, they have divine power to demolish strongholds [*to stand up to the Shadow Voice*]. We demolish arguments and every pretension that sets itself up against the knowledge of God, and we take captive every thought to make it obedient to Christ" (2 Corinthians 10:4–5).

Likewise, in his letter to the Romans, Paul instructed them to be "transformed by the renewing" of their minds (Romans 12:2). In another letter to the Philippians, he encouraged these folks to focus like a laser on what was uplifting, right, pure, healthy, and encouraging (Philippians 4:8). Take every thought captive. Renew your mind. Think on things that are excellent, praiseworthy, and true. The point is clear. You have a responsibility for what to think about, and to think on that which is true.

Perhaps you are saying to yourself, "That's great, but how do I do that? How do I stand up to my Shadow Voice? How am I supposed to stand up to and take captive these destructive, self-condemning thoughts that enter my mind?"

As a clinical psychologist and pastor, Dr. William Backus has helped thousands of men and women deal with the vicious cycle of negative self-talk with his "Misbelief Therapy." Dr. Backus laid down a simple yet profound three-step method to help people capture their thoughts and beat the Shadow Voice at its own game. I've adapted his method below and added a bonus step that will help you confront and overcome these negative, condemning thoughts that attempt to thwart you from surviving the day. The following steps can change your attitude and your ability to make it through any brutal day that you will face.[2]

STEP ONE:

PAY ATTENTION TO WHAT YOU'RE TELLING YOURSELF

Right now, as you read these words, you have a thought loop going in your mind. If you could pause for a bit and get quiet, you'd notice that your mind is still working. It's telling you things. You may be wondering, *Will this method work for me?* Or, *How will these three steps apply to my unique situation?* Or, *What if they don't work for me? What will I do then?* Right now, you're talking to yourself in your mind, and you're drawing conclusions based on those thoughts.

Over the course of our lives, we all have difficult circumstances and disappointing experiences. Challenging events happen, and in an attempt to survive them, we start telling ourselves things about each event. And what we tell ourselves may be just as important as the facts of the event itself. For example, if a romantic relationship just ended or you lost your job, it's not just the facts of those events that matter. What you tell yourself about the breakup or the job loss will impact how you process the facts and create lasting impressions about yourself that will shape your future. Your interpretation of those facts will influence how you live the rest of your life.

Let's look at the breakup scenario. Most of us have experienced a broken heart at the end of a romantic relationship. So let's say someone breaks up with you. Maybe your ex didn't have the courage to do it in person and just texted you (that is pretty weak and lame). As a result, you feel devastated. You begin to wonder what went wrong. Then you begin telling yourself such things as *I must have done something wrong*. Very quickly that thought spirals down to *Maybe something is wrong with me. I must be flawed. I'll never be loved again. I must be unlovable.* And you see how that doom loop turns from the facts of the event that happened, a relationship that just didn't work out, to your interpretations about your own self-worth. That's the Shadow Voice at work.

So what happens when we start paying attention to our inner dialogue, this conversation going on inside of our minds unsupervised? We notice the conversation. We become aware of things we're telling ourselves that are simply false. They're misbeliefs, but we typically don't recognize them as unhelpful and untrue and filter them out. We don't stop and label them as wrong and counterproductive. No, we just accept them as truth.

And we start to believe these half-truths, these lies, and they have damaging effects on our mental and emotional health and life in so many ways.

The first thing we have to do is to pay attention to the internal dialogue that has been on autopilot for most of our lives. We have to recognize the running, often negative narrative we have going on inside of our minds. One way to begin this process is to actually take inventory of our thoughts by writing them down. I've got a little red notebook I use to capture my thoughts. I also have a running Word doc on my computer where I record my inner world. This way I get it outside of myself. Once I do this, I can look at my thoughts objectively, then do something about them. Find your own way in a journal, on your phone, or whatever works best for you. Capture what you're telling yourself by recording the thoughts you notice.

In order to stand up to the Shadow Voice, we must first pay attention to what we're telling ourselves and how we are interpreting the events in our lives. Getting a grip on our thoughts and misbeliefs will lead us to more freedom in our lives.

STEP TWO:

AGGRESSIVELY ARGUE WITH THESE MISBELIEFS

My daughters were cheerleaders in high school. Cheerleading has definitely evolved since I was in school. It is now very athletic, and the cheerleaders are pseudo gymnasts. It's much more of a competitive sport than it used to be. In order to try out, my daughters had to learn to do flips and all kinds of different gymnastics moves. I had to pay extra coaches to help them learn how to do these acrobatics so they could make the team. Back when I was in school, the most important thing about cheerleading was a loud voice and an ability to learn the cheers. It wasn't about tumbling and flips. They had cheers, and a certain cheer is still ingrained in my mind. "Be aggressive, b-e aggressive. B-E, A-G-G-R-E-S-S-I-V-E, hey, hey, aggressive." Be aggressive! When it comes to this second step in standing up to the Bully Brain, you must be aggressive.

If we are going to survive the day and confront the Bully Brain mentality, the second step is to argue with these false beliefs and lies. We have to be aggressive, B-E, A-G-G-R-E-S-S-I-V-E, in dealing with these negative thoughts. We must deal aggressively with the bully thoughts that come into our hearts and minds.

In order to win the battle against your misbeliefs, you're going to have to argue aggressively. Argue when you wake up in the morning. Argue when you're trying to go to sleep at night. Anytime these thoughts come racing through, you have to take issue with them. You must win the argument. I'll tell you how in step three.

Let's say you're in charge of a project at work that you invested a lot of time and energy into. Maybe the project didn't turn out the way you or your boss wanted it. Maybe you got called to the table on it. That inner dialogue shows up immediately. Your first thought is *Wow, what went wrong?* And the next thought is *Maybe I did something wrong.* And then you think, *Maybe I don't have what it takes to do the job. What am I going to do next? I'm probably going to lose my job. Then I'm not going to have enough money to pay the bills. I'm a loser.* The worst-case scenario just hijacked your day—again.

But it doesn't have to! You can take charge of your thoughts by recognizing that they are simply not the truth. You can intervene and change the narrative. You've got to argue with those thoughts—or "cast down arguments" as Paul would say (2 Corinthians 10:5 NKJV). You may or may not have done a good job on the project. But guess what? You're human. You may have made a mistake. Correct the mistake. Get better, improve. That's the truth. The fact of the matter is we all fail once in a while. We all make mistakes, and most of the time we learn more from our mistakes than we do from our successes. We can even use mistakes as stepping-stones. Now is the time to talk back to the negative accusations.

How can you do that? You can say to yourself, "I'm not a loser because I made one mistake. I feel like I blew it at work, but God is still with me. Today is a new day. Just because one relationship didn't work doesn't mean I won't find love in the future. I'm not unlovable. That's just not the truth. That's not a fact. What matters is God loves me. God really loves me. God deeply cares for me and He is with me. I may be upset. I may be brokenhearted. I am still a child of God." That is how you can argue aggressively with the lies and false beliefs of the Shadow Voice.

Think about the people in the Bible. Think about Peter. He denied Christ one, two, three times. What if Peter kept telling himself, "I'm a failure. I'm a loser. I'm a betrayer. Now I can't be a leader anymore. I can't do this anymore"? What if he listened to those thoughts over and over again?

What about Paul? Can you imagine the negative thoughts that could have stopped his ministry? "You killed Christians. You had Christians thrown in jail. How can you say you're a Christian? Look at your past. How can you say you're a pastor?" Moses killed an Egyptian. He wasn't the best spokesman. The accusing voice in his head must have said, "You're a murderer. You can never lead God's people. You can't even speak well. Who would want to listen to you?" Abraham's Shadow Voice would have reminded him, "You lied. You're a liar. No one can ever trust you again."

We could go on and on with the major heroes of the Bible. If we look in Hebrews 11 at the people listed in the faith hall of fame, we see that all of them were flawed. And I'm sure they all had to argue aggressively against the thoughts of condemnation that would roll into their minds again and again and again. We have to do the same thing.

We have to stand up to the Shadow Voice. The first step is to pay attention to what we are telling ourselves. Externalize, write it down, and take inventory of the negative talk. The second step is to argue aggressively with the misbeliefs. Then we are ready for the third step, which we find in Romans 12:2: "Do not conform to the pattern of this world, but be transformed by the renewing of your mind."

STEP THREE:

SPEAK THE TRUTH TO YOURSELF

Once you identify the Shadow Voice inside your mind, you can argue against its running monologue. But that's not enough. Now you have to replace the misbeliefs with truth.

Dr. Martyn Lloyd-Jones tells us how to do this in his book *Spiritual Depression: Its Causes and Cures*: "I say that we must talk to ourselves instead of allowing 'ourselves' to talk to us! Do you realize what this means? I suggest that the main trouble in this whole matter of spiritual depression in a sense is this, that we allow our self to talk to us instead of talking to our self. Am I just trying to be deliberately paradoxical? Far from it … Have you realized that most of your unhappiness in life is due to the fact that you are listening to yourself instead of talking to yourself?"

Dr. Lloyd-Jones continued to talk about the importance of telling ourselves the truth, and he gave some practical advice: "Take those thoughts that come to you the moment you wake up in the morning. You have not originated them, but they start talking to you, they bring back the problems of yesterday, etc. Somebody is talking. Who is talking to you? Your self is talking to you. Now [the psalmist's] treatment was this; instead of allowing this self to talk to him, he starts talking to himself. 'Why are thou cast down, O my soul?' he asks. His soul had been depressing him, crushing him. So he stands up and says: 'Self, listen for a moment, I will speak to you.... Why art thou cast down?'"[3]

We see this three-step method replete in the book of Psalms. The psalmist wrote down his negative and condemning thoughts and his battles against them in argument form, and then he spoke the truth to himself that God was still his Rock, his Shepherd, his Strength in times of troubles. I turned to the Psalms every day for months and years to survive my storm. I read Psalm 86 every morning. I prayed it, I memorized parts of it, and I would look to it throughout my day. It was my way of combating the Shadow Voice. Like David did, I fought the lies with the truth of God's Word.

Even though I am no longer in the most intense part of my storm, I still keep the practice of this three-step method. In fact, while writing this chapter, I began to struggle with feelings of resentment. I woke up one morning convicted that I didn't want this resentment to grow and fester inside of me. I wrote down some of my internal dialogue. I started replacing it with truth, and I composed it into a note on my phone. The first part of it was "Resentment is poison. Holding on to resentment and holding on to grudges is poison. You think you're hurting the other person, but you're just poisoning yourself." Then I wrote "Resentment is poison" on my phone calendar for that day.

Later, after a few days had passed, I wrote, "Well, what's the antidote to that? What's the truth? It's true that resentment is poison, but forgiveness is freedom. Forgiveness is freedom, and I want to live that out. I want the truth that resentment is poison and forgiveness is freedom to be lived out in my life."

We replace these lies and misbeliefs with the truth. That's the renewing of our minds. That's focusing on what is right, what is true, what is excellent, what's worthy of praise. And this is something we have to do over and over and over again. The good news is we have a choice.

No matter what happened to you, you have a choice to renew your mind on who God is and what God says about you. You have a choice to reject misbeliefs coming into your mind and to accept and incorporate what is true and right and life-giving into your mind. You can choose to focus on truths that line up with God's Word and what He says about you.

We all have a choice and a responsibility to do that. We can't control things that happen to us. We can't control our circumstances or other people. But we can control our responses to them. We can stand up to the Shadow Voice and begin to control what we allow in our minds. God gave us the ability to do that. Isn't that great?

Anytime you start getting worried or anxious about something, an alarm should go off automatically. *Beep, beep, beep.* Check yourself. *I'm getting anxious, I'm getting worried. What is it I'm telling myself about this situation?* Notice that you're having thoughts of hopelessness about your life, about where you're going. You can acknowledge that thought but then realize it can't be from God. Then you know you've got to replace it with God's truth. *I know God is with me. I know God is for me, not against me, and I am His child. I am who He says I am.*

BONUS STEP:

RINSE AND REPEAT

Stop and take an internal selfie. Write down the thoughts going through your mind. What are the misbeliefs and lies you've been telling yourself? Then argue with these misbeliefs. Take issue with them. Challenge them. And then, third, speak God's truth to yourself. And then rinse and repeat. Dr. Leaf stated, "Thoughts are real, physical things that occupy mental real estate. Moment by moment, every day, you are changing the structure of your brain through your thinking. When we hope, it is an activity of the mind that changes the structure of our brain in a positive and normal direction."[4]

You may want to keep these steps close to your heart and mind. Write them down. Live them out. You'll want to go back to them time and time again because the mind gets messy. Just like you take out the trash at home, you must take out the trash in your mind. Otherwise, it can have a horrific impact on your life. You may want to go through these three steps with a friend or perhaps a counselor.

If you have decided to survive the day with the power of God on your side, then you can become who He designed you to become. You can tear down those strongholds. You can take every thought captive. What a powerful concept! Speak to yourself, instead of allowing your condemning and worrying self to speak to you. Try that out today. Clean up the dorm room of your mind. Practice healthy thinking by preaching the truth of God's love, power, and presence to yourself when you experience resentment, guilt, or depression. He is with you always. He loves you so much that He sent His Son to die in your place.

Be aggressive, be proactive, but be patient. God is with you, and God will help you root out negative thoughts, destructive patterns, and the strongholds that threaten to bring you down. Why? Because He is the God who created us and loves us. He is the God who redeems our souls, our hearts, and our minds. How? By giving us His truth to replace the destructive lies. "You will know the truth, and the truth will set you free." (John 8:32) And "if the Son sets you free, you will be free indeed" (John 8:36).

SURVIVAL PRAYER:

Father, I choose to get a grip on my inner dialogue today and what I am telling myself. Help me to replace the lies with Your truth. Thank You that because of Christ I am accepted, loved, and empowered to live a new life.

SURVIVAL PASSAGE:

> For though we live in the world, we do not wage war as the world does. The weapons we fight with are not the weapons of the world. On the contrary, they have divine power to demolish

strongholds. We demolish arguments and every
pretension that sets itself up against the knowledge of God, and we take captive every thought
to make it obedient to Christ.

2 Corinthians 10:3–5

SURVIVAL PRACTICE:

Write down the lies and misbeliefs you are telling yourself. Argue
against those untruths. Write down the truth, and tell yourself
that truth.

CHAPTER ELEVEN

STOP COMPARING

"Comparison is the thief of joy."

Teddy Roosevelt

Most of us are familiar with the term *binge watching*. We can now watch hours and hours of our favorite show back to back, season by season, in one night or over a weekend. Writers know just the right tension and uncertainty to create the perfect cliffhanger in the last five minutes of the show that compels us to watch the next episode. "Just one more," we tell ourselves at 8:00 p.m., until we look up and it's 1:30 a.m. and we have to get up and go to work in a few hours! Binge watching has its perils. We love these shows because we get invested in the characters' lives and the dilemmas the writer places them in. The uncertainty and sense of incompletion leave us longing for more. We binge watch because it feels impossible to stop.

Recently, I was bingeing on some lighthearted comedy when I came across a YouTube sketch of iconic comedian Bob Newhart, who gained international fame playing a therapist on his eponymous TV show back in the '70s. In the sketch, a client named Katherine comes to see him with a load of problems. Her main issue is the fear of being buried alive in a box. Before the session begins, Newhart warns her that he gives his patients only five minutes and charges only five dollars and does not give change. She pours out her fears about being buried alive in a box, about struggling with an eating disorder, and about having toxic relationships with men.

Newhart listens empathetically, pauses, then leans over and abruptly says, "STOP IT!"

"That's it?" Katherine asks.

Bob repeats, "STOP IT!"

Katherine then asks if he wants to delve into her childhood, and Bob responds, "Oh no. We don't go there. Just STOP IT!"[1]

Being in the helping profession my entire life and having sat through hundreds of sessions on therapist couches myself, I can relate to this episode. Of course, it's an oversimplification and a parody on counseling, but there is a kernel of truth and even genius to it. There are some things in life that we must simply *stop doing* if we are going to make it through the day. There are also some things we must *start doing* to make it through the day. It's one thing to hear "STOP IT!" delivered by a comedian in a six-minute sketch; it's quite another thing to hear the same words delivered by someone who's been there.

Tracy Barnes is one of my heroes of the faith and a man who knows the ins and outs of survival. Tracy and his wife, Debbie, possess a type of wisdom and knowledge about surviving the day unlike few people I've ever met. In the fall of 1986, the Barneses discovered their seven- and three-year-old sons both had a genetic condition known as Duchenne muscular dystrophy, which essentially means their muscles were slowly wasting away. At that moment, Tracy and Debbie knew their lives had taken a dramatic turn. Their family would never be the same. The doctor told them that the boys would only live to about nineteen years of age.

Despite the dire circumstances, Tracy and Debbie committed themselves to survive the day in a way that would reflect the power and grace of God in each of their lives. Today, their "street cred" stems from decades of helping, serving, and sacrificing behind the scenes just to keep their two sons, Roger and Phillip, alive.

Debbie described what their typical day looked like taking care of one of their sons. "If he wants to get up in the morning, you have to get him up. You have to literally pick him up and put him in his wheelchair. You pick him up and put him on the toilet. You have to shave him. You have to cut his fingernails. You have to scratch his head for him." As time went on, each of the boys lost the ability to care for themselves in any way. Toward the end of Phillip's life, he even lost the ability to swallow. He was dependent on Debbie to suction his mouth repeatedly just so he wouldn't choke or drown in his own saliva. Their selfless, diligent, and tender care continued seven days a week, every week of the month, every month of the year for close to thirty years before Roger and Phillip went on to be with the Lord.

Debbie shared how this reality impacted her. "There was a time years ago where I was so overwhelmed by the fact that my two sons had this disease, that I was mad at God. I pulled into myself. I was angry, and I spent a while there. But then, as time went on, I realized, *What good is that? And Why am I turning my back on God, the only one who can help me?*"

Debbie and Tracy don't speak about their journey of survival with God often, but when they do, I listen and take notes. Why? Because they've been through such a long, difficult trial and yet they still have great joy in their lives. I want to know the secret to that! Tracy talks with earned authority about what you must *stop doing* when you are faced with dire circumstances. Whether it's caring for a special-needs child, going through a divorce, dealing with a mentally ill loved one, or trying to cope with an addiction, his advice is invaluable. With their permission, I have paraphrased and adapted Tracy and Debbie's game-changing advice on how to survive the day. I've also thrown in some steps I've learned as well.

Here are *three stops* and *three starts* that are essential survival skills when life gets hard.

1. STOP COMPARING

If you are going through a battle (such as cancer, major financial troubles, or your spouse left you), it's easy to start comparing your life to the lives of other people. You look around at friends who are in perfect health, or others who don't have to struggle financially, or family members who have wonderful marriages and successful kids, and you start to ask, *Why? Why me? Why are they thriving and I am struggling? Why can't I catch a break like they have? Why am I stuck in this painful mess and they seem to have it all?* Life is unfair; just take a look around.

It's true. Life is unfair. It can even be relentless and brutal. But comparing your life to others' lives will not help you move forward and survive the day. Comparing will not help your attitude or your ability to make it through today. Your struggle is yours. Your life storm is yours. Your whole life is yours and no one else's. Wishing, envying, and comparing your Instagram posts to others' will only bring heartache. Playing the comparison game will only make you bitter, depressed, and angry. If you catch yourself comparing, just stop it and ask God for the grace to move forward.

President Theodore "Teddy" Roosevelt, who overcame much adversity in his own life, said, "Comparison is the thief of joy." Comparison robs you of deep joy and diverts your attention away from the very life God has given to you.

2. STOP COMPLAINING

When you're faced with arduous circumstances that will remain with you for the long haul, it's easy to fixate on your situation. When you talk to or text a friend, you pour out how difficult your life is, how hard every single day is, and how nobody really understands what you're going through. No one wants to be around people who are always dumping their problems on them or whining about their pain. Granted, you are in a tough season that may extend way out into the future, but everyone around you doesn't need to hear about that every day. If you are always complaining, you will find yourself alone and isolated.

Save all your complaining for God, in your journal or in your prayers. Lay it all out before Him—your woes, your pain, your ongoing problems. Pour it all out to God and perhaps a counselor or a support group. But don't turn your friends and family into your personal 911 emergency help center. It will wear them out and it will not help you deal with issues of your day.

3. STOP CAVING

When my life fell apart and rumors swirled around my community every single day, I wanted to just withdraw into a cave. I wanted to isolate myself from others and especially social gatherings. I wanted to stay home and skip church because I felt like a leper (probably not a good decision since that's where I work). When dealing with an ongoing life storm, it's so easy to want to retreat into your cave.

When Elijah was on the run from Jezebel, he was afraid and depressed, so he hid in the cave at Horeb. God called him to come out of the cave and into the light. He knew Elijah needed to connect to people he loved, and Elijah needed to get back into the game (1 Kings 19).

You were created for community, for interaction with others, not for isolation and cave dwelling. Withdrawing from church, from friends, from work, from hobbies is the worst thing you can do. I know it's a temptation to do that, but don't! Stop withdrawing and stop isolating yourself from community. It's when we are hurting and struggling that we need community the most. That's how God designed it.

Most of these stop signs are negative. Stop comparing. Stop complaining. And stop caving. But they are necessary negations to make positive progress. Even grace teaches us to set some healthy boundaries and "nos" in our lives. "For the grace of God has appeared that offers salvation to all people. It teaches us to say 'No' to ungodliness and worldly passions, and to live self-controlled, upright and godly lives in this present age" (Titus 2:11–12).

To win in team sports you need a good offense and a good defense. Some say that a good defense is what wins championships. Think about these three stops as a strong, healthy defense that will help you stall the negative progression and get your offense back on the field.

At the same time, you need to score some points. So the following are three starts, your offense, that will help you make it through the day.

1. START THANKING

The apostle Paul had to be one of the most grateful people who ever lived. Though he suffered gravely, endured hardships throughout his life, and even had a mysterious thorn in his side that never went away, Paul practiced gratitude. In one of his most memorable passages, writing from the confines of a prison cell, he documented these words, "Be anxious for nothing, but in everything by prayer and supplication, with thanksgiving, let your requests be made known to God" (Philippians 4:6 NKJV). In other words, Paul said the secret is to lay it all out before God, thank Him, and trust in His strength to live through you.

Having taken Paul's admonition to heart, I got on my knees by my bed every morning for years and thanked God for everything I could think of before my feet hit the floor. I started by thanking Him for the pillow, the bed, the roof over my head, and the foundation that held up my house. I thanked Him for the construction workers filling the potholes in the streets, for firemen, policemen, our mayor, and the people on the city council. I thanked Him for coffee, bagels, and the clothes I wore. I thanked Him for friends, family, and the church. I thanked God for everything I could think of until my "thanker" wore out. Then I got up to take on the day. At night, I repeated the same prayer of thanks before I went to sleep.

It turns out I wasn't the only one with that practice. A good friend of mine, who's now thirty years sober, started his journey to freedom and sobriety by getting on his knees in the morning and thanking God for helping him not drink that day and then ending each day back on his knees, thanking God for helping him to stay away from alcohol. When he first started this prayer of thanksgiving years ago, he was an atheist, which is a little ironic. Over time, as he pretended to believe in God, he realized God was actually there and was the one who kept him free from drinking.

How much more power and strength does God have for you? You probably know God is there, but perhaps you have not tapped

The **ART OF LIVING**

THANKFULLY GIVES

us the **PERSPECTIVE**

and **POWER**

to **FACE ANY DAY**.

into this power of living a grateful life. If you've never done so before, I invite you to start today.

When we thank God for all things, He begins to empower us with joy and contentment. When we are thankful, our desire to compare our lives to others is quelled and we begin to take on our days and our lives with fresh eyes. Humility includes the awareness to thank God for our very existence and dependence on Him. Thanking God is also a way of living out grace, receiving with gratitude the blessings in life that He gives to us that we do not deserve. The art of living thankfully gives us the perspective and power to face any day.

2. START CARING

Another way to positively fight the temptation to compare, complain, and cave is to start caring for someone else. It is easy for us to be self-focused, especially during a crisis. But looking outside of ourselves is a great way to get unstuck and move forward. We need to be open to spontaneous and long-term acts of kindness and caring. Opportunities are all around us, even in the strangest of places.

Tony Campolo is a rare combination of sociologist and preacher. He has taught and spoken around the world for decades, raising money for Haiti and the inner cities of the United States. He once told a story about an unorthodox act of spontaneous kindness.

He was asked to speak at a conference in Honolulu, Hawaii. Due to the time-zone change and jet lag, he was unable to sleep and left his hotel to find a diner at 3:30 in the morning to get something to eat.

While he was there, a group of boisterous prostitutes came in and sat down at a table nearby. One young woman named Agnes proclaimed to the group that tomorrow was her birthday. All of her friends chided her and made fun of her because of her abrupt announcement. Agnes spoke up again, "Hey, take it easy. I just wanted you to know. I'm not expecting you to throw a party or anything. I have never had a party in my life. Why would I want one now?"

After the prostitutes left the diner, Campolo asked the owner if the same group came in every night. The man behind the counter said, "Yup." Then Campolo got the wildest idea to throw a surprise birthday party for Agnes. At 2:30 the next morning, Tony and the owner decorated the place and baked a special birthday cake for Agnes. When she waltzed through the door around 3:00 a.m., she was stunned. She was so moved by the gesture of love that she broke down in tears. She didn't eat the cake but immediately took it home to save it, only to return to the party later.

When Agnes left, Campolo found himself surrounded by prostitutes. Taken aback by the awkward moment, he decided to pray. He prayed for Agnes, her birthday, and all of her friends holding hands in that awkward moment in that old diner. After the prayer, the owner blurted out, "Hey, you never told me you were a preacher! What kind of church do you belong to anyway?" And Campolo replied, "The kind of church that throws birthday parties for prostitutes at 3:00 in the morning."

What a gesture. We should always be open to unexpected opportunities to look at other people's lives and see their needs rather than our own.

3. START SERVING

If you research common methods for helping cure depression, you will find all kinds of studies, theories, and medical solutions. There are so many diverse treatments that claim to help with depression. However, in the myriad of experts, there's a near unanimous consensus that the following two actions will help you if you are feeling depressed:

1. Spend time outside walking or jogging. Even when that's the last thing you want to do.
2. Start serving others in some capacity. Serving others is at the heart of surviving the day.

In the ultimate act of humility, God came from heaven down to earth. He humbled Himself, took up a towel, and washed the feet of His followers. Jesus told His disciples He "did not come to be served, but to serve, and to give his life as a ransom for many" (Matthew 20:28).

God intended for us to follow the example of Jesus and designed us to serve other people. There are so many ways we can do that. All you have to do is start small and start somewhere. Go to your church, find a pastor, and ask a simple question, "I want to do something to serve. How can I help?" Go to the Salvation Army and ask the same question, "I want to do something to serve. How can I help?" Go to a crisis pregnancy center and ask the same question. Go to Habitat for Humanity and repeat the question. You get it.

There is a place for you to start serving. I know the pain and challenge you feel right now are real and omnipresent. I get it. I've been there, and I'm still there on some level. But whenever I get focused on my needs, my problems, and my pain, life gets really dark. I am not living the way God set things up. He made us to serve. We are saved in order to serve. All you have to do is be open and you will find a place to serve.

I recently had dinner with some new friends who moved across the country from Chicago to Florida. While in Chicago they served their local church in the blended-families ministry. They both had full-time jobs but served many hours a week at their church. Both had endured a massive amount of pain, suffering, and disappointment in their own broken lives, but they were committed to serving. And they knew the benefit of giving back. When they moved to Florida, they searched for a church where they could get involved and serve. Once they found one, they jumped in headfirst and started a ministry to help mentor couples in blended families. As we shared our meal together, they beamed with the joy of having found another place to serve. Their joy was contagious. It warmed my heart to listen to their story and see their passion for serving despite the pain and complications of their own lives.

I urge you to find a place to serve in your church or your community. I promise you will be amazed at what your efforts will do for others and, surreptitiously, for you as well.

We were not created to compare, complain, and cave as we move through this life storm, as these things will only weigh us down. We were created to live a life of thanksgiving, caring, and serving—these are strategies that will make a radical, life-changing difference. Coupled with humility, grace, and surrender, there's great practical power in this offense and defense of starts and stops.

SURVIVAL PRAYER:

Father, show me the areas in my life that I need to *stop* and actions I need to *start*. I want to live a life of sincere gratitude and service for others. Thank You for the breath in my lungs today and the opportunity I have to serve others.

SURVIVAL PASSAGE:

> Do not be anxious about anything, but in every situation, by prayer and petition, with thanksgiving, present your requests to God. And the peace of God, which transcends all understanding, will guard your hearts and your minds in Christ Jesus.

Philippians 4:6–7

SURVIVAL PRACTICE:

Make a list of all the things you are thankful for today.
Make a plan to serve someone else today with an act of kindness.

CHAPTER TWELVE

TEN ESSENTIALS FOR SURVIVAL

"All the world is full of suffering. It is also full of the overcoming of it."

Helen Keller

Throughout this book I've used the pronoun "we" for the most part because we are all in this thing together. We either have survived tough days or are trying to survive tough days right now, but we have all been there at some time or another. But in this final section, I have switched to the second-person voice, "you." My first book ever published was *The Ten Commandments of Dating* with Dr. Sam Adams. It's an easy-read, self-help, sarcastic kind of work written to people in the dating scene. We took a common-sense, matter-of-fact approach to relationships. In honor of that form, I want to give you *The Ten Essentials for Surviving the Day*. I could have said "The Ten

Commandments," but considering all that you have on your plate right now, "commandments" seems a little harsh.

Note, I am not trying to add a list of things for you to do today. You may be thinking, *Oh no, humility, grace, surrender, and now a list of ten more things! You've got to be kidding me.* Well, on one hand I am and on the other hand I am not. These essentials helped me and many other people make it through tough days; therefore, I know they can help you. Perhaps you can just do one essential today and that's enough. Check it off your list. Then do another one tomorrow.

ESSENTIAL ONE:

DO SOMETHING TO MOVE FORWARD

Baby steps. This is a biggie. Do something that will make you move forward with your life. Whether that's reading a book, attending a seminar to improve your skills, learning a new language, getting an online degree, do something productive and life-giving. Take an action that moves you forward and keeps you from living in the past or in the land of regrets. If you get stuck thinking about the past, challenge yourself to take one step forward today.

If you **GET STUCK**

THINKING about the **PAST,**

CHALLENGE YOURSELF

to **TAKE ONE STEP**

FORWARD TODAY.

ESSENTIAL TWO:

GET OFF THE COUCH AND GO OUTSIDE

Even if you live in the Arctic Circle or the Sahara Desert, get off the couch, turn off the TV or computer, and go outdoors. Go for a walk, a jog, or a bike ride, and move your body outside. Get in a workout. Skip around the block. Swim a few laps. Run in the park. Choose something you'd enjoy and just get moving. Step outside and breathe in nature. Feel nature all around you—the heat, the rain, the snow, the wind. Listen, I am not some granola guy; I love to hang out indoors. But I know there's power in spending time outside every day. Try it and see what happens for you.

ESSENTIAL THREE:

JOURNAL LIKE A MADMAN

My counselor told me to journal, and it made such a difference for me that now I'm recommending it to you. Write in a journal as if your life depends on it. Buy a spiral notebook or a leather journal, open a Word doc or type in the notes app on your smartphone. Choose whatever medium you like, and start writing. Get all the anger, the pain, the frustration, the disappointment outside of you by scribbling out your emotions.

Don't worry what it looks like. Regardless of your penmanship, you'll be in good company as you write. I've done a lot of journaling myself. Jerry Sittser journaled. David's psalms look like journaling. So journal your heart out. Vomit on the page. Cry on the page. Laugh on the page. Cut and paste quotes if you want to, or verses, prayers, great advice people gave you, and stupid advice people said to you. Journaling is good therapy.

ESSENTIAL FOUR:

MAKE YOUR BED

Admiral William McRaven wrote an entire bestselling book titled *Make Your Bed* in which he talked about the implications of one positive action in the morning.[1]

Plus, it's tough to make a bed when you are still sleeping in it. Jordan Peterson, clinical psychologist and public intellectual, has an entire chapter in his book on making your bed and cleaning your room.[2] How can you stop climate change if you don't even change the sheets on your bed? Do some small stuff. Then move forward.

ESSENTIAL FIVE:

GO TO WORK TODAY

Work is critical to your mental and emotional health. God designed us to work, to be useful to others. Work gives meaning to our lives and structure to our days. And it usually involves money, which allows us to eat, drink water, and have shelter. Plus, at work you will interact with people, hopefully face to face. You gotta go to work today. It's crucial. If you aren't in the workforce at this stage of life, find someplace to volunteer! Being of service in a job or as a volunteer is good for your soul.

ESSENTIAL SIX:

TALK TO SOMEONE TODAY

You need to actually talk to someone on the phone or in person every day. Texting and emailing and Facebooking or Instant Messaging does not cut it. There's no substitute for real face time or FaceTime or Skype or conversation over coffee. We need human interaction. It's healthy and necessary. God made us that way, especially when we are going through some tough stuff. Call someone. FaceTime someone. Get coffee, grab lunch or dinner. Schedule an activity with someone. You get the point.

ESSENTIAL SEVEN:

ATTEND A MEETING

Find a group of people who are going through the same struggle you're going through. If you are grieving, find a grief support meeting. If you are an addict, attend an AA meeting. If you are codependent (dealing with someone else's addiction or mental illness), go to Al-Anon. If you or someone you love is dealing with mental illness issues, find a NAMI (National Alliance on Mental Illness) group near you. Going through a divorce? Attend a divorce recovery group. It helps to know you are not alone in the survival battle and to receive wisdom from people who are further down the road than you.

ESSENTIAL EIGHT:

LAUGH ABOUT IT

Laughter really is the best medicine. Sometimes it helps to laugh at the absurdity of it all. I am not making light of what you're going through in the slightest. I only want to point out that we all have options; we can laugh or we can cry. Some days I laugh. Other days I cry. And still other days I do both. But maintaining a sense of humor is helpful and healing. If you have a hard time finding something funny to laugh about, try watching a Brian Regan or Jim Gaffigan stand-up comedy clip on YouTube.

ESSENTIAL NINE:

SIMPLIFY YOUR LIFE

Determine what you can do to simplify your life to the bare essentials. What must you do today? You have to work. You have to eat. You have to sleep. You have to keep your body moving. You need to practice humility, grace, and surrender, of course. Declutter your home or your office if you need to. Get the heck off of social media. Don't watch or read the news for a while. Simplicity helps to clear the pressure and noise in your head. There is peace to be found in simplicity.

ESSENTIAL TEN:

HELP SOMEONE ELSE TODAY

There's a whole wide world of people out there who are hurting and need your help. Do something to help a friend, a family member, or even a stranger. Get your focus off yourself and your circumstances by doing something for someone else. Send a text to a friend and let them know you're praying for them. Call and encourage them. Volunteer in your local soup kitchen or food pantry. Visit an elderly person in a nursing home. Go help someone.

Look at the list of essential practices. Get up and move forward with this day. If you can't do all ten today, don't sweat it. Write it down or put it in your calendar to do it tomorrow, but whatever you do, take action so you don't get stuck. Here's the list of essentials again:

1. ESSENTIAL ONE: DO SOMETHING TO MOVE FORWARD
2. ESSENTIAL TWO: GET OFF THE COUCH AND GO OUTSIDE

3. ESSENTIAL THREE: JOURNAL LIKE A MADMAN

4. ESSENTIAL FOUR: MAKE YOUR BED

5. ESSENTIAL FIVE: GO TO WORK TODAY

6. ESSENTIAL SIX: TALK TO SOMEONE TODAY

7. ESSENTIAL SEVEN: ATTEND A MEETING

8. ESSENTIAL EIGHT: LAUGH ABOUT IT

9. ESSENTIAL NINE: SIMPLIFY YOUR LIFE

10. ESSENTIAL TEN: HELP SOMEONE ELSE TODAY

In the opening of this book, I asked you to imagine trying to cross a raging river to make it to the other side. You took that challenge listening to all the guides on the other side encouraging you to pay attention to the Stronger Voice, to choose humility, grace, and surrender. These three powerful choices will bring the strength and wisdom of God into your life as you follow Him one day at a time. And these ten essentials will help! I promise. Remember, I am not just the Hair Club for Men president; I am also a member. Like you, I'm a bona fide member of the Pain Club.

I discovered that these three choices not only help me make it through my darkest day, but they truly help me make it through life. I will never arrive at a place in this life where I do not need humility, grace, and surrender. These words are God's platform that allows us to hear His Stronger Voice and to do His will. I pray that you will take them to heart, put them into practice, and begin to thrive despite your circumstances. I'll see you on the other side.

SURVIVAL PRAYER:

Father, I choose to move forward with my life today. I can do nothing to change the past, but You can redeem the past as I move forward today. Help me to get my eyes off myself and onto others. I know You are with me and will guide me through.

SURVIVAL PASSAGE:

> Finally, brothers and sisters, whatever is true, whatever is noble, whatever is right, whatever is pure, whatever is lovely, whatever is admirable— if anything is excellent or praiseworthy—think about such things. Whatever you have learned or received or heard from me, or seen in me— put it into practice. And the God of peace will be with you.

> *Philippians 4:8–9*

SURVIVAL PRACTICE:

Take a walk today or do something that will get your body moving—jogging, swimming, or working out. Movement is healing!

GOING DEEPER

Use these questions in a group discussion or write your own answers and thoughts in your journal.

CHAPTER ONE:

WHAT ABOUT BOB?

1. Describe the life storm you're trying to navigate right now.

2. "You can't control the storm, but you can control your response." What could controlling your response look like in the context of your life?

3. Name some experienced "guides" you can turn to in order to make it to the other side of the river. Who can you reach out to today?

CHAPTER TWO:

DROWNING TODAY

1. Pain, stress, loss, and disappointment often hit us like waves. What waves are crashing on your life today?

2. Describe a time when you found yourself disoriented in life. What emotions did you feel at the time?

3. Think back to a previous tough time in your life. Where did you look for guidance? What sources proved to be the most helpful to you?

4. Read Psalm 69:1–3. How did David describe his time of crisis, and where did he turn for help?

CHAPTER THREE:

FAILURE PLUS

1. What is your instinctive reaction to a trial? Is it to fight or take flight? What does that usually look like?

2. How have your experiences of pain, loss, or disappointment made you feel like a failure? Why do you think we blame ourselves for things that happen that are out of our control?

3. Of the responses to pain, which do you find yourself defaulting to? In what ways has that response let you down?

CHAPTER FOUR:

YOUR SHADOW VOICE

1. Name the three parts of the personality according to Carl Jung. If you dig deep, what are a few of the things about yourself you might have hiding in a box?

2. What are the tactics the Shadow Voice uses to keep us feeling trapped in our troubles? What recording does it play on a loop in your mind?

3. Of the different ways we can hear the Stronger Voice, which one speaks most clearly to you?

CHAPTER FIVE:

WHEN THE PAIN REMAINS

1. What does it mean that God's no is also His yes?

2. Jesus tells us He is humble and gentle of heart. Do you see Him in that way?

3. Describe a situation when you experienced God's power in your weakness.

4. What does it mean to bring your thorn to the throne? When God allows our thorns to remain, what does He promise to do for us instead?

5. Describe a time when God gave you a "ticket" of grace at just the right moment.

CHAPTER SIX:

CHOOSING GOD'S JIU-JITSU

1. In light of reading this chapter, how would you define *humility*?

2. What are some advantages of humility in relationships with others? In your relationship with God?

3. How does humility benefit us?

4. Describe someone you know who is "down to earth." What do you admire about that person?

CHAPTER SEVEN:

UNEXPECTED LOVE

1. Can you recall a time when you received a gift you didn't deserve? How did that make you feel?

2. What has your personal experience of grace taught you about God's love for you?

3. What does it mean to accept God's radical acceptance? How might that make a difference in your life right now?

4. Read Ephesians 2:8–10. In what ways can you daily remind yourself of this truth? How might you preach the gospel to yourself every day?

CHAPTER EIGHT:

ESTAMOS CONTENTOS

1. What is the key to contentment, and why is it such a difficult thing to achieve?

2. Can you point to a situation in which you had a healthy influence on someone? How did that differ from a time when you sought to control something or someone?

3. Is there something or someone in your life that you need to surrender? What would keep you from letting go?

4. Read Psalm 55:22: "Give your burdens to the LORD, and he will take care of you. He will not permit the godly to slip and fall" (NLT). What does this passage say about letting go and trusting "the catcher"?

CHAPTER NINE:

WIN THE MORNING

1. What can a sunrise tell us about our suffering?

2. It's important to put ourselves in position to turn difficult circumstances to our advantage. What gestures or positions can we use to physically demonstrate humility, grace, and surrender?

3. Think about how Jesus demonstrated humility, grace, and surrender. What strikes you most about His choice to respond this way?

4. Read 1 Samuel 7:12. *Ebenezer* means "stone of help" and is a tangible reminder of God's faithfulness. Looking back at your life, name some instances where you could place your own Ebenezers.

CHAPTER TEN:

SILENCING YOUR SHADOW VOICE

1. Do you keep a journal? How could writing about your trials help you process them?

2. What are the lies or misbeliefs that you are telling yourself?

3. What is the truth you need to speak back to yourself to replace the lies?

4. Is there someone you can share your inner dialogue with who can help you sort out the lies and the truth?

CHAPTER ELEVEN:

STOP COMPARING

1. Take an honest look in the mirror. In what areas do you compare your circumstances to those of others? What do you find yourself complaining about? How often do you think of the needs and feelings of others more than your own?

2. How difficult do you think it would be to *stop* doing those things?

3. Name the three things you can *start* doing now to help you survive the day. Make a list of specific ways you can do those three things in your life today.

CHAPTER TWELVE:

TEN ESSENTIALS FOR SURVIVAL

1. Which of the "essentials" do you find easiest to do? Which do you find more difficult?

2. If you were going to start a new project or set a new goal today, what would it be?

3. In what ways do you think journaling can be a healthy and helpful practice?

4. What will you do differently *today* to help you survive the day?

ACKNOWLEDGMENTS

Surviving the day was not and is not a solo task. It takes a family, it takes a village, it takes a community. I dedicate this book to my precious daughters, Nicole and Claire, who know better than anyone how to survive and thrive in the midst of life's storms. I love y'all so very much.

Deep thanks to my wonderful wife, Krissie, who masterfully wrote all the study questions for this book. I love you intensely, and the redemption story continues! It was only through the help of parents, my brothers Ed and Cliff, Tim Mavergeorge, Dr. Julia Prillaman, Dr. Jerry Sittser, and Dave Riggle that I survived long enough to write this book. I am forever indebted. Thanks to Esther Fedorkevich for the fresh angle on this book and to Tori Thacher and Toni Richmond for reworking the manuscript to make it better. I am grateful to the team at David C Cook, especially Michael Covington, Nathan Landry, Jack Campbell, and particularly the expert editing skills of Alice Crider.

NOTES

CHAPTER TWO: DROWNING TODAY

1. See Ben Young, *Room for Doubt: How Uncertainty Can Deepen Your Faith* (Colorado Springs: David C Cook, 2017); and Ben Young, *Why Mike's Not a Christian: Honest Questions about Evolution, Relativism, Hypocrisy, and More*, 3rd ed. (Dallas: Creality Publishing, 2013).

2. See Walter Brueggemann's examination of Paul Ricoeur's philosophy in *The Psalms and the Life of Faith*, ed. Patrick D. Miller (Minneapolis: Fortress Press, 1995), 24.

3. Søren Kierkegaard, *Journals IV A 164* (1843). Full quote: "It is perfectly true, as the philosophers say, that life must be understood backwards. But they forget the other proposition, that it must be lived forwards."

CHAPTER FOUR: YOUR SHADOW VOICE

1. David E. Schoen, *The War of the Gods in Addiction: C. G. Jung, Alcoholics Anonymous, and Archetypal Evil* (New Orleans: Spring Journal Books, 2009), see esp. ch. 3, "An Exploration of Archetypal Shadow/Archetypal Evil as an Essential Ingredient in Addiction."

2. *Life Today TV*, Randy Robison interview with Scott Hamilton, February 15, 2018, www.lifetoday.org/video, or www.youtube.com/watch ?v=8woGLRC4HCQ.

CHAPTER FIVE: WHEN THE PAIN REMAINS

1. *Shadowlands*, directed by Richard Attenborough (Price Entertainment, 1994).

2. John Blanchard, *Truth for Life: A Devotional Commentary on the Epistle of James* (Welwyn, United Kingdom: Evangelical Press, 1986), 268.

3. Corrie ten Boom, *The Hiding Place* (Grand Rapids, MI: Chosen Books, 2006).

CHAPTER SIX: CHOOSING GOD'S JIU-JITSU

1. Jordan B. Peterson, *12 Rules for Life: An Antidote to Chaos* (New York: Random House, 2018).

CHAPTER SEVEN: UNEXPECTED LOVE

1. Gerald G. May, *Addiction and Grace: Love and Spirituality in the Healing of Addictions* (New York: HarperOne, 2007).

2. Jerry Bridges, *The Discipline of Grace: God's Role and Our Role in the Pursuit of Holiness* (Colorado Springs: NavPress, 1994).

3. Walter A. Elwell, ed., *Evangelical Dictionary of Theology* (Grand Rapids, MI: Baker Books, 1984), 316.

4. Richard Foster, foreword in James Bryan Smith, *Embracing the Love of God: The Path and Promise of Christian Life* (New York: HarperOne, 2008), xiii.

CHAPTER EIGHT: ESTAMOS CONTENTOS

1. Alex Lickerman, "Influence vs. Control: Though Control Is Denied Us, Influence Is What We Need," *Psychology Today*, January 1, 2012, www.psychologytoday.com/us/blog/happiness-in-world/201201 /influence-vs-control.

2. Chris Sandel, "About Us," Seven Health, accessed June 20, 2019, https://seven-health.com/about-us/.

3. Melody Beattie, *More Language of Letting Go: 366 New Daily Meditations* (Center City, MN: Hazelden, 2000), January 13 entry.

4. Original credit for flyer and catcher illustration to Henri Nouwen in his *Henri Nouwen: Writings* (Maryknoll, NY: Orbis Books, 1998).

CHAPTER NINE: WIN THE MORNING

1. Mark Twain, "Letter to Gertrude Natkin," March 2, 1906, accessed February 24, 2020, www.twainquotes.com/Compliment.html.

2. Tim Ferriss, interviewed by Chase Jarvis, "Win the Morning. Win the Day," YouTube video, January 19, 2017, www.youtube.com /watch?v=9nO4wFbdNx0. See also Tim Ferriss, *The 4-Hour Workweek: Escape the 9–5, Live Anywhere, and Join the New Rich* (New York: Crown, 2009).

3. Jerry Sittser, *A Grace Revealed: How God Redeems the Story of Your Life* (Grand Rapids, MI: Zondervan, 2012), 130.

CHAPTER TEN: SILENCING YOUR SHADOW VOICE

1. Caroline Leaf, prologue, *Switch On Your Brain: The Key to Peak Happiness, Thinking, and Health* (Grand Rapids, MI: Baker Books, 2015).
2. William Backus and Marie Chapian, *Telling Yourself the Truth* (Bloomington, MN: Bethany, 2000).
3. Martyn Lloyd-Jones, "General Consideration," chapter 1 in *Spiritual Depression: Its Causes and Its Cure* (Grand Rapids, MI: Eerdmans, 1965).
4. Leaf, *Switch On Your Brain.*

CHAPTER ELEVEN: STOP COMPARING

1. Bob Newhart "Stop It!" sketch, *Mad TV*, season 6, episode 24, May 12, 2001.

CHAPTER TWELVE: TEN ESSENTIALS FOR SURVIVAL

1. William H. McRaven, *Make Your Bed: Little Things That Can Change Your Life … and Maybe the World* (New York: Grand Central, 2017).
2. Jordan B. Peterson, *12 Rules for Life: An Antidote to Chaos* (New York: Random House, 2018).

BIBLE CREDITS

Unless otherwise noted, all Scripture quotations are taken from THE HOLY BIBLE, NEW INTERNATIONAL VERSION®, NIV® Copyright © 1973, 2011 by Biblica, Inc.® Used by permission. All rights reserved worldwide. The author has added italics to Scripture quotations for emphasis.

Scripture quotations marked ESV are taken from the ESV® Bible (The Holy Bible, English Standard Version®), copyright © 2001 by Crossway, a publishing ministry of Good News Publishers. Used by permission. All rights reserved.

Scripture quotations marked KJV are taken from the King James Version of the Bible. (Public Domain.)

Scripture quotations marked THE MESSAGE are taken from THE MESSAGE. Copyright © by Eugene H. Peterson 1993, 2002. Used by permission of Tyndale House Publishers, Inc.

You Are Not the Only One Who Doubts

In *Room for Doubt*, Ben Young shares his story of doubt in his journey toward God. Together, you will explore the myths we believe about faith and why it's normal to be disappointed with God. Learn about giants of the faith who wrestled with uncertainty and proved there is room for doubt in the life of faith.

Available everywhere books are sold.

DAVID C COOK
transforming lives together